Date Due

BRUA 83		
MAR 0 1 1986		
MAY 2 9 1990		
FEB 1 4 1991		
MAY 2 1 1992		
DEC 08 '95		

Ethnic
Folk Costumes
in Canada

Ethnic Folk Costumes in Canada

Peggy Tyrchniewicz

Photographs by
Bill Hicks

Hyperion Press Limited
Winnipeg Canada

Copyright 1979 Hyperion Press Limited

300 Wales Avenue, Winnipeg, Manitoba, Canada R2M 2S9

All rights reserved

ISBN: 0-920534-10-4 (cloth)

ISBN: 0-920534-11-2 (paper)

Design by A. Osen

Map illustrations by Dori Taite

Photography by Bill Hicks Design and Photography Ltd.
61 Gertie Street, Winnipeg, Manitoba

Typeset by Derksen Printers, Steinbach, Manitoba

Color Separations by GB Graphics Ltd.
1249 Gateway Road, Winnipeg, Manitoba

Printed and bound by D. W. Friesen and Sons, Ltd.
Altona, Manitoba, Canada

Printed in Canada

The Author

Peggy Tyrchniewicz is Associate Professor, Department of Clothing and Textiles, Faculty of Home Economics at The University of Manitoba. Her life-long interest in textiles led her first to a B.Sc. (H.Ec.) in 1963 and later to a M.Sc. in 1972. Historic costumes and Canadian dress became her special areas of study and she has pursued this research all over the world. She has also been active on the Department's teaching staff for many years and has served as Acting Head of the Department. Born and raised in Russell, Manitoba, she now lives in Winnipeg with her professor husband, Edward, and two sons, Allen and David.

The Photographer

Bill Hicks is a specialist in commercial and industrial photography and has his own studio, Bill Hicks Design and Photography, Ltd., in Winnipeg. After leaving the University of Manitoba School of Art he developed his photography hobby into a successful business. Although he has long been interested in ethnic culture and ethnic dancing, the photographs in this book represent his first professional attempt to capture the spirit of ethnic folk art as it is represented in traditional dress. He is now photographing other aspects of Canadian life and culture. He has lived in Winnipeg all his life.

Contents

Foreword

Costume, in its most obvious sense of clothing, is one of the fundamental needs of man. But it can be and often is much more. It can be a highly developed art governed by fashion, or a folk-art perpetuating the age-old traditions of a people. It is in the latter sense that this book deals with the subject. Moreover the present study deals with costume which is native to various parts of the world, but which has been brought to Canada by the peoples of various cultures who have settled within our boundaries. The costume of our native peoples indigenous to North America lies outside its scope.

As a nation with two founding cultures we should naturally expect to see the early transference of the fashions of seventeenth- and eighteenth-century France to the towns of New France and those of eighteenth- and nineteenth-century England into the towns of British North America. That is what happened; but there were also adaptations of the everyday dress of ordinary men to suit the needs of the Canadian farmer, *coureur de bois*, lumberjack, and cowboy.

All this was only to be expected. What was unexpected by our earlier settlers was that the railway age and the industrial era should bring such a massive influx of peoples from all quarters of the globe: at first the eastern, northern, and southern Europeans and then Orientals, Africans, and Latin Americans. Among these, certain highly cohesive groups such as the Ukrainians have been particularly tenacious of their customs, arts, and costume. But the others have also contributed to the mosaic that is the Canada of today.

Multiculturalism inevitably poses problems to the modern nation-state; and some nations today are frightened of pluralism. Canada, however, accepts multiculturalism as a part of her very nature and is determined to fashion a new kind of nation out of diverse elements. Her challenge and her ideal are to create, as in any great work of mosaic art, a highly varied design within the strong boundaries of unity. This book illustrates the importance of costume as an element in the colourful composition of our culture today.

His Excellency the Right Honourable Edward Schreyer
C.C., C.M.M., C.D.
Governor General of Canada

Preface

My love affair with beautiful textiles led me to admire and appreciate the exquisite folk costumes worn with such pride by so many Canadians. At first I was intrigued by the variety of fabrics. The handwoven linen and wool, the luxurious satins, velvets, and brocades, the hand embroidery, the lovely laces, and the fingerwoven belts had a fascination I could not ignore. Later, I began to appreciate the care with which the fabrics had been used. From the detail of complicated garment construction, the fascinating use of color and texture, the superb workmanship, and the careful way in which the garments were treated I began to understand the love and pride that people feel for their ethnic dress. As I traveled to other countries and was exposed to private and museum collections of ethnic dress and as I visited festivals where folk costume is worn with such obvious enthusiasm, I was fascinated by the history of the costumes and the interest they generate for wearers and viewers alike.

In this book I have tried to share my joy of discovery with you. The research represents my rewarding pursuit of folk costumes among the ethnic groups in Canada. It has been a pleasant undertaking. I've met people from all walks of life and many countries of the world who share with me the love of ethnic costumes. Their pride in their national dress and their enthusiasm for the preservation of their cultural heritage is overwhelming. Everywhere I was confronted with knowledgeable people who were eager to tell me about old country customs and costume details. I have learned from these people. Many have shared their deep understanding of life with me, and I have benefited from knowing that hopes and joys, fears and sorrows touch all of us in much the same way no matter where we live or what language we speak. In many cases, their talking about ethnic costumes brought back feelings of distant homelands and led to an appreciative evaluation of life in Canada. To these great people I am indeed indebted.

The information I have presented here represents an exploration of ethnic dress seen in Canada. It is at best a brief summary of a detailed and complicated subject. There are many ethnic groups in Canada, and I have tried to contact those who have costumes available. Some groups had so many variations of costumes from each town or village of their homeland that I could not possibly acknowledge every different outfit. I tried to choose a representative selection from these areas. Where there was a distinctive national dress from a country my problem of selection was made easier. If there were several outfits worn for different occasions or by different classes or groups I tried to explain these variations. More women's costumes than men's costumes appear in the book. This is not because men were less co-operative or enthusiastic about my project but because not as many authentic men's costumes have been brought to Canada. Ethnic dance groups, churches, and cultural centers across Canada were the source of much information. They provided many costumes and I learned that it is through their efforts that ethnic traditions and ethnic costumes are being preserved.

My research has been concentrated on ethnic dress as it is worn and used in Canada. I have tried to present an accurate picture of what is seen in Canada today. To make the description clearer I have added some background details about each country and tried to trace a brief outline of the history of the costume in that country. I do not pretend that this book is a history of costume or a complete representation of the costumes of any country. Rather, I hope the book will remind all Canadians of their rich and varied heritage and make them proud that so many different peoples now call Canada their home.

Many people have been involved in the production of this book. To each of them I extend my thanks. I am especially grateful to those who posed in their costumes for photographs. Without them, this book could not have been made. I must also thank Bill Hicks for his splendid photography and for his skill and patience in getting just the right pose. I am indebted to the publishers of this book who suggested the idea to me and who have worked tirelessly to see the book reach completion. My thanks also to those at the Community Folk Arts Council of Winnipeg who supported us in this endeavor and helped find contacts with the various ethnic groups in Canada and encouraged their participation in this project. I am grateful to members of The University of Manitoba, especially the Faculty of Home Economics, who have supported and encouraged me and who have allowed me the time and the freedom to pursue my interests in this exciting area. I also acknowledge, with thanks, the assistance towards typing I received from The University of Manitoba and the Social Sciences and Humanities Research Council Fund Committee. My special thanks to Jo-Anne Doig who suffered through reading my handwritten copy to type this manuscript and to Marion Gaucher who helped research the material.

Finally, I would like to record my appreciation and my love to my family and friends who gave me generous encouragement and support through all the ups and downs of collecting the material and writing a rough draft. Without the love and backing of my husband Edward, my sons Allen and David, and my special friends Peggy and Chuck Framingham this book would never have been completed.

Introduction

This Land is your Land,
This Land is my Land

What other country can claim such spectacular features as the Rocky Mountains, Niagara Falls, rugged coastlines of three oceans, expansive prairies, the northern tundra, large inland lakes, rushing rivers, and peaceful streams. The immense size and variation of the land alone inspires pride in country. But this spectacular scenery pales before the uniqueness of the people. Canada's population is an international mosaic; nearly all the ethnic origins of the world are represented in the blend that is Canadian. Within the last five hundred years this country has changed from a sparsely populated new world frontier to an exciting multicultural nation. Canada is almost entirely populated by immigrants and descendants of immigrants. Only three hundred thousand native people indigenous to North America currently live in Canada, but they, too, make a valued contribution to the Canadian mosaic.

Canada has benefited in all ways from the mixture of so many cultures. In the areas of understanding and tolerance, knowing about and appreciating another lifestyle can help ease prejudice. Learning that language differences, social skills, economic circumstances, and traditional ideals can affect the understanding and solution of a problem makes everyone aware of individual differences and individual rights. No matter if we are Christian, Hindu, Buddhist, Muslim, or Jew; no matter if we come from Europe, Asia, Africa, or South America; no matter if we pursue the sciences or the humanities, all people achieve fulfillment in an atmosphere of mutual trust and acceptance. Each of us brings his own background and experience to daily tasks. If by sharing our resources we can achieve a new vision and a new perspective we will become a great nation.

Canada has not always welcomed different ideologies. What prevents complete acceptance of the different ways of life? Often, it is fear of the unknown or a firm belief that the way we know is the best way. We are suspicious of people who talk differently, dress differently, and eat differently. We see and resent only the differences and we have no patience to find out what things we have in common. Some immigrant groups have been used as scapegoats, and we have blamed them for our problems. We have found the cause of unemployment in the numbers of low status immigrant groups or the numbers of married women who wish to work, not in the complicated issues of an industrialized society. Canada is still a young country; we are still learning to value our rich and varied heritage.

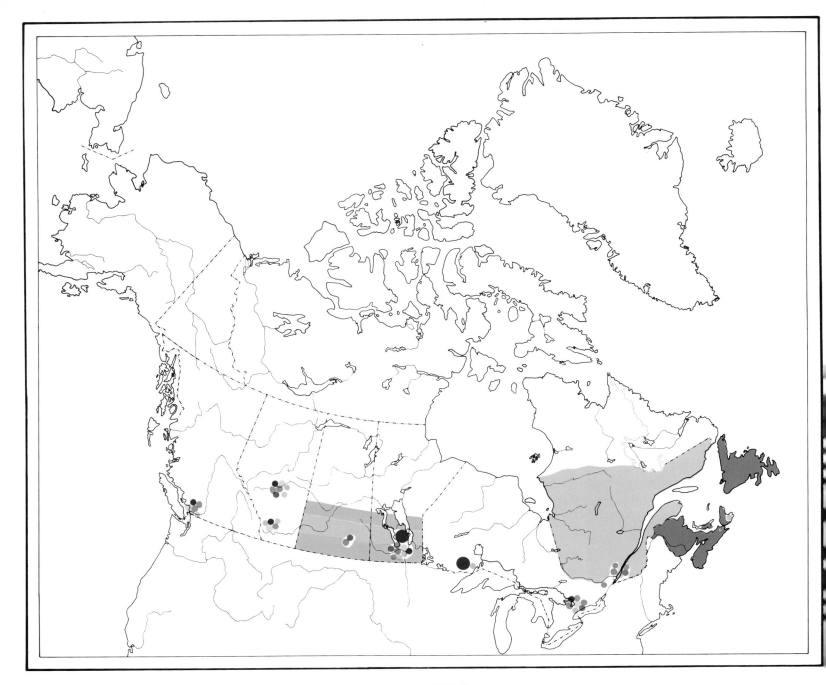

Asian countries have settled in major cities across Canada:
China (Vancouver, Calgary, Edmonton, Winnipeg, Toronto, Montreal)
India, Korea, Japan, Pakistan, and the Philippines follow this same pattern.

Balkan States
Croatia (Toronto, Vancouver)
Greece (Ontario, Quebec)
Romania (Montreal, Toronto, Winnipeg, Regina, Edmonton)
Serbia (Toronto)

Baltic States and Eastern Europe
Estonia (Winnipeg, Edmonton, Toronto)
Latvia and Lithuania (Montreal, Toronto, Winnipeg, Vancouver, Nova Scotia, and rural prairies and rural Ontario)
Hungary (Montreal, Toronto, Calgary, Vancouver)
Czechoslovakia
Czechs (Toronto, Vancouver, Edmonton, Calgary)
Slovaks (Toronto, Montreal, Thunder Bay)
Poland (generally across Canada, Toronto, Winnipeg, Edmonton, and Vancouver)
Russia (Vancouver, Montreal, Toronto, Calgary, Edmonton)
Ukraine (Prairies, Winnipeg, Edmonton, Toronto)

British Isles
England, Ireland, Scotland, and Wales have settled across Canada.
Ireland (Montreal, Toronto)
Scotland (Maritimes)

Scandinavia
Denmark across Canada
Finland (northern Ontario, Toronto, Thunder Bay, Vancouver)
Iceland (Interlake-Gimli, and western provinces)
Norway and Sweden (Vancouver, Edmonton, Calgary, Winnipeg, Toronto)

Western Europe
French (Quebec, Winnipeg)
Germany (Vancouver, Edmonton, Toronto, rural prairies)
Italy (Vancouver, Montreal, Toronto)
Netherlands (Vancouver, Edmonton, Calgary, Winnipeg, Toronto)
Portugal and Spain (Toronto, Montreal, and Winnipeg)

Middle East
Israel (major cities across Canada)
Lebanon (Montreal, Toronto, Calgary)

South America
Chile (Winnipeg, Regina, Edmonton)

Caribbean (Toronto, Ottawa-Hull, Montreal, Winnipeg)

When we celebrated our first Centennial as a nation in 1967, we began to look at the cultural contributions the ethnic groups had made to our Canadian identity, as well. As everyone was encouraged to celebrate Canada's birthday, small ethnic groups began holding festivals and inviting their neighbors to experience their traditions of song, dance, and foods. We began to see that ethnic and Canadian went well together.

In the very heart of Canada, in one of the areas of the greatest mix of peoples from many ethnic origins, many groups joined together to create a large folk festival called Folklorama. Each participating ethnic group established a pavilion where they displayed and demonstrated items representing their cultural heritage to thousands of enthusiastic observers. For an entire week a city of half a million people, almost a mini United Nations in its diversity, immerses itself in its rich traditions and finds its true identity. So popular was the festival that it has become an annual event and now attracts participants and observers from around the world. Similar festivals are beginning to happen around the country. In Toronto, Caravan is very popular.

Besides the large multiculture festivals in Canada, many exciting single culture festivals are also world renowned. Winter Carnival in Quebec, Pioneer Days in Saskatoon, the Scottish Festival in Charlottetown, the Sourdough Rendezvous in White Horse, the Six Nation Pageant in Brantford, John Cabot Day in Cape North, the Toonik Times Spring Festival in Frobisher Bay, Discovery Day in Newfoundland, the Danish Folk Festival in New Denmark, Klondike Days in Edmonton, Islendingadagurinn in Gimli, and many many more are celebrated with enthusiasm. From Vancouver Island to Bonavista Canadians are recognizing and appreciating the enrichment that comes from the diversity of cultures that is the heritage of all of us.

One of the most obvious features of the festivals is the dress. The colorful, often elaborate costumes tell us a great deal about the culture of the participator. Some countries have established a national dress or a costume that is or was worn by nearly all members of the society. The sari in India is a national dress. Although there are many other costumes worn in India, nearly every female has a sari. In other countries, similar yet distinctively different dress has been established in each small district. This has happened throughout most of Europe and the Scandinavian, Baltic, and Balkan States. The costume is known as regional dress. Both national and regional dress may also be known as folk costume.

Folk costume describes the outfits that have been accepted by a region or country as an outfit that has been traditionally worn. In Europe, the trend toward folk costume started in the sixteenth century when the lower classes began to prosper and could afford to copy the fashionable dress of the upper class, albeit in a modified form. The fashionable dress was modified to suit rural requirements and the ability of the people to obtain the fabrics and decorations. In trading areas, foreign laces and fabrics became popular, whereas in isolated areas local resources had to supply their tastes. Because of the limited resources of some of the people and their rural location, the styles did not change every year. Garments that represented a substantial amount of individual effort or money spent were worn for years and often handed down for generations. Eventually a style became static within an area and traditions held it to be the one true costume. With industrialization and improvement in living standards, modern western dress became more acceptable and the folk costumes were preserved only for special occasions. When the occasion came, however, everyone, upper and lower class alike, wore the folk costume with nationalistic pride. Some

time later the costume began to be less favored, even for special events, and the outfit became a festival dress, worn only for festivals that celebrated the traditional ways of the country. Thus, the costume progressed from the peasant dress of the rural people, to folk costume recognized for the country or region, and finally to festival dress for cultural celebrations.

The folk costumes worn in Canada today represent the costumes worn in the homeland. Some representations are more authentic than others. Some people have access to the traditional fabrics and decorations and can obtain the necessary pieces to complete the costume; others must make do with the materials available in a modern Canadian store. Some folk costumes are made from layers of handwoven wool and are too warm to wear in the heat of Canadian summers. These must be changed to accommodate the climate. Not always the most lavish and expensive costumes are copied in Canada. Often, too, highly stylized or greatly modified costumes are used. These are all part of the folk costume of Canada.

Various ethnic groups in Canada are also at different stages in their acculturation process. Folk costume, if it was worn in the homeland, is often worn by the immigrant in his new home. Children are reared in the old traditions and dressed in the folk costumes in spite of the fact their dress may attract attention in their community. These second generation Canadians are not as well trained in the ethnic traditions and often do not realize the value of perpetuating them. First generation Canadians spend their time learning the Canadian culture and learning to prosper in it. They, too, put traditions aside even though they recognize and regret the weakening of old ties. The third generation, however, usually feels comfortable enough in the Canadian environment and have the confidence to seek their cultural roots and try to preserve the traditions of their origin. This is helped by the interest in individual heritage now becoming a national focus. New Canadians are urged to believe that their traditions must be upheld for the sake of their own culture and for the entire Canadian heritage. Lord Tweedsmuir, former Governor General of Canada, addressed his remarks to Ukrainian Canadians but they apply equally to all ethnic groups.

You have accepted the duties and loyalties of, as you have acquired the privileges of Canadian citizens, but I want you also to remember your old Ukrainian traditions — your beautiful handicrafts, your folk songs and dances, and your folk legends. I do not believe that any people can be strong unless they remember and keep in touch with all their past. You will all be better Canadians for being also good Ukrainians . . . .

Another difference between ethnic groups in Canada is detected between those that came from politically stable countries and those that left their homeland during times of tension. As war approaches, nationalistic feelings intensify. This is often shown in the increased use of regional or national dress. As people leave the country in anticipation of war, they take with them strong emotions about their home country which is evidenced in their use of costumes in Canada. Often the new Canadians still associate with their former homelands and not with the political reality of today. Because this book is focused upon the Canadian people, I have

tried to take their feelings into account and identify
the individuals to their homelands as they have known
them. They have told us their story and we have allowed
them to choose their own costumes for the photographs.
They were asked to bring their folk dress and they
brought those garments that they wore in their homeland or that they wear now to festivals in Canada.

This book is organized to include the major ethnic
groups represented in our country. The two founding
cultures are discussed first. Unfortunately, the native
and Métis populations had to be left for another study.
The diversity and detail of the outstanding costumes of
the many tribes were too extensive for this volume.
Next to be discussed is the mosaic of cultures that form
the Canadian cultural heritage. For convenience they
have been arranged under geographical areas of the
homeland; for example, Asians, Balkans, Baltic, British
Isles, Eastern Europe, Western Europe, and others. Within each group the countries have been arranged in al-
phabetical order. The costumes in the photographs are
identified by names where possible and placed in geo-
grahic areas. The names of the models are listed at the
back of the book.

1 Founding Cultures

England
France

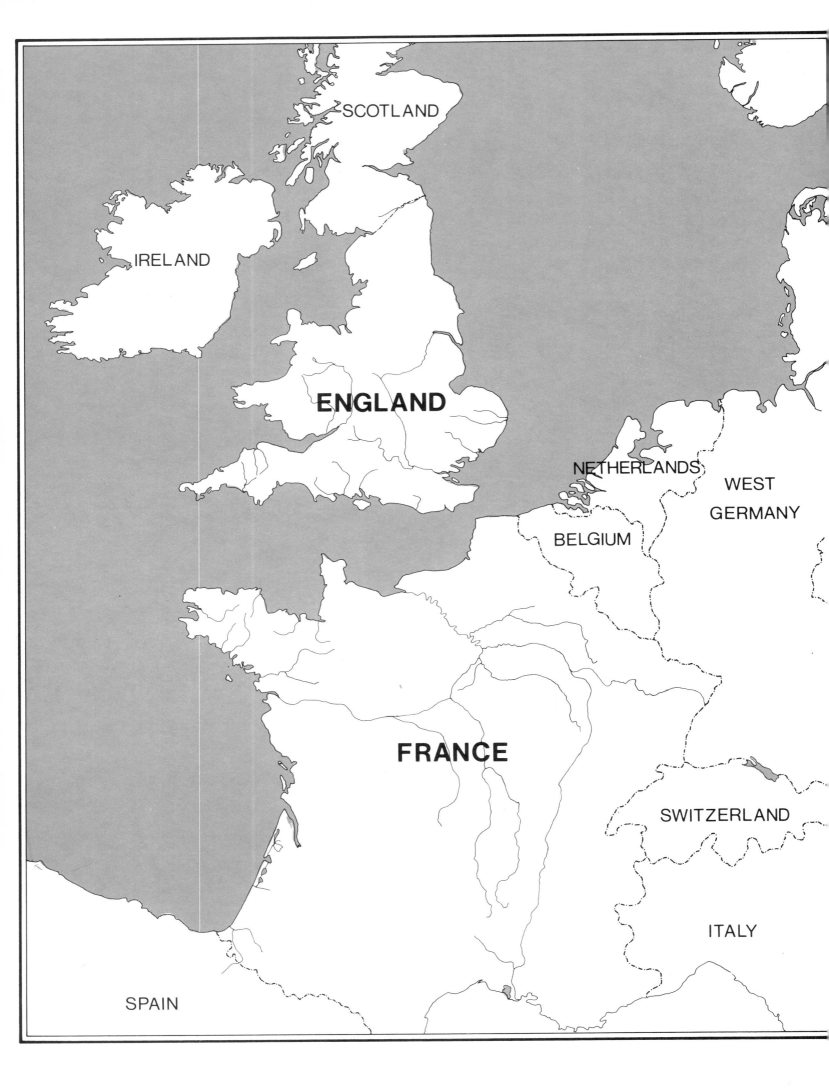

French and English have been the two predominant cultures of Canada. The two great traditions have co-existed side by side throughout Canada's history. Although some customs have been shared, it has been more usual that separate traditions have been maintained which have developed new concepts along individual lines. Neither culture has maintained a strong tradition of folk costume since arriving in Canada. In part, this is because there was not a strong tradition of folk costume in either homeland. French settlers came to Canada before the French folk costume was thoroughly established in France, and in any event the new Canadians soon lost contact with their fellow countrymen. Most of the English settlers arrived wearing modern western dress. Since they maintained close contact with their countrymen they regularly received the latest fashion advice from home. Their attention was focused on adaptation of current fashion trends. Today, with renewed interest being expressed about ethnic costumes, French and English Canadians have attempted to trace their early folk costume traditions. French Canadians have turned to their early Canadian dress styles for the folk costumes for their twentieth-century festivals and dance groups. The English have focused upon a modified version of early fashionable dress and a specific dance costume as a representation of their national dress.

Traditionally, French and English Canadians have settled in different areas of the country. The French have favored Quebec, where seventy-nine percent of the total population is French. Seventy-seven percent of French Canadians live in that province. As one moves farther west there is a smaller French Canadian population. Twelve percent of French Canadians live in Ontario; nearly four percent live on the prairies, mostly in a small section of Manitoba; and only one point six percent live in British Columbia. Nearly five point six percent live farther east in the Atlantic provinces. Those people of English origin favor Ontario where forty-seven and a half percent of English Canadians live. Just over sixteen percent live in both the Atlantic provinces and the prairies. Thirteen percent live in British Columbia and only six point six percent live in Quebec. Both English and French migration began in Canada before the major immigration movements after World War II.

England

As one of the founding peoples of Canada, the English have contributed greatly to Canadian culture. Their presence has been felt in the Canadian region since the beginning of the sixteenth century when the early explorers first started to investigate the eastern shores of this newly discovered land. In 1670, with the incorporation of the Hudson's Bay Company, the English established a permanent contact with the area. Since that time, English immigration has been slow but steady. A large influx of English settlers arrived here in the eighteenth century. These were the United Empire Loyalists who emigrated from the United States. Not all the Loyalists in this group were English. In fact they represented people from all over Europe who had had favorable experiences under the British crown and who chose to maintain English ties. Now, English Canadians have penetrated every region and aspect of Canadian life. Over six million Canadians list English as their ethnic origin.

So much of the Canadian culture is identified as English in origin that it is often assumed that any part of the culture that is not specifically French has its roots in English. Actually, Canadian culture is a blending of many cultures and it becomes increasingly difficult to identify the truly English aspect of it. When one looks at history in retrospect the contributions that England has made to the world are remarkable, especially when one realizes that constitutionally England does not even exist. The Act of the Union in 1707, swallowed England into the larger entity of the United Kingdom. Since then, Scotland, Wales, and Ireland have all been more successful than England in retaining their national identity. In recent years, concern has been raised about the speed at which English traditions are being forgotten and obliterated within the modern society. Recently, efforts have begun to restore the old English customs and landscape.

In Canada, the song, dance, and dress of Merry Old England are being preserved by the Royal Country Dance Societies. Such dance groups are now popular across the country. Although special English festivals are not yet held in Canada, there are a number that go on in Eng-

1 A modern adaptation of early nineteenth-century dress is worn for English country dance in Canada. Homemade costumes are the most usual.

land. Witman Day, Harvest, Mid Winter, and May Day festivals are among those celebrated.

English Canadian folk dress is worn for sword and country dancing. The costume chosen for the dance is some form of dress from the royal courts that was in style in the past. High fashion is not a criterion and no particular time period is adhered to. The dancers prefer a time period that features a full skirt that would be comfortable for dancing. Late eighteenth-century and early nineteenth-century dress is a popular choice. The outfits are a general statement about the time and are characteristic of most areas of England. Regional differences of costume, although they existed in the past, are not reflected in the dance dress today.

In England it was traditional for families to make their own outfits rather than hire the services of a tailor. This tradition has often been maintained in Canada. The man's and woman's costumes illustrated in photograph 1 have both been recently made for country dancing. The printed red dress has an empire waistline and a deep skirt frill. The U-shaped neckline and lower sleeve are trimmed with narrow white lace. The sleeves are slightly gathered at the upper armscye. With this comfortable dress, a petticoat and small black shoes are worn. The man's outfit includes well tailored wool breeches and vest which are both trimmed with brass buttons. The breeches and vest may be made from any dark fabric available such as cotton, linen, velveteen, corduroy, or wool. Brass buckles are also used to tighten the breeches just below the knees. A white shirt with a wrist frill and center front jabot is made from cotton. Handknit white wool socks are worn with dark dress shoes. This costume is appropriate for country dancing and also for sword dancing.

Another popular form of male English folk dancing is morris dancing. Traditionally, only men do this colorful and lively dance, but during periods of war women have taught young boys and in this way the dance has been kept alive. The costume for this dance consists of white shirt and long trousers, usually cotton. The baldrick crosses at both center front and center back. The leg bands are bell pads that jingle when the men dance.

2   This morris dancer wears the customary white costume and bells. The vigorous English dance tradition is carried on in Canada by English country dance societies.

Handkerchiefs and sticks are carried and waved. The arm bands and neckerchief are local additions to the costume for color. Usually a cricket cap is worn with the outfit. Since this dance is often performed at sports events, dancers often use team colors for decoration. The colors of the baldrick cap and any other added adornments are personal choices. The costume illustrated in photograph 2 is from the Headington region and uses green and yellow. The rosette design at the cross in the baldrick is repeated at center back and on the arm bands.

It is encouraging to see renewed interest in English traditions. England has had a tremendous influence on the world during the last four hundred years. It seems appropriate to preserve some of the folk traditions of the country.

France

The French were the first Europeans to immigrate into Canada and establish permanent residence here. They are one of the founding groups of our great Canadian nation and their effect on Canadian culture has been beneficial and far-reaching. Today, people of French ethnic origin make up twenty-nine percent of the Canadian population. The largest concentration of French Canadians is in Quebec, where they comprise seventy-nine percent of the people there. There is also a substantial settlement around the St. Boniface area of Manitoba and others in the Atlantic provinces. Ontario, too, has many small French communities along its eastern borders.

The people of French ethnic origin in Canada have been residents in Canada for generations. The first farmer, Louis Hebert and his wife, son, and two daughters came to Canada with the intention of homesteading in 1617. In those early days immigration into Canada progressed slowly. Most of the immigrants were men who came to Canada looking for adventure and wealth as they explored the wilds and traded furs. A greater French influx occurred during the time that Jean Talon was Intendant of the new colony between 1666 and 1672. He was determined to make the struggling French colony self-sufficient and part of his plan was to encourage families. Many single French girls, whose dowery was supplied by the King of France, were brought to Canada to marry the men homesteading in the settlements. After Talon's recall to France, French immigration into Canada decreased until 1759 when the French were defeated in the battle on the Plains of Abraham and Canada came under British influence. Since then there has been only minimal emigration from France.

The clothing of French Canadians reflects a different time period than most other ethnic dress worn in Canada. French settlers came to Canada in the seventeenth century and brought with them peasant dress and upper class dress, depending on their status at that time. The folk dress of European countries had not yet crystalized into the static costumes that became recognized as national dress. Therefore the French Canadian dress developed to its current state in Canada rather than in France. The costume styles reflect the peasant dress of France, but the outfits more closely resemble the modern

3 Traditional French Canadian peasant dress has been adopted by many French Canadian folk dance groups such as Les Danseurs de la Rivière Rouge. For winter wear, a warm cloak or capot would also have been worn by early French Canadian settlers.

dress worn in Canada during the last three hundred years. Styles of ethnic dress in France developed along different lines. For example, dress became more complicated and made use of expensive fabrics such as handmade laces, velvets, and brocades which were all produced in regions of France. Headdresses, too, became extreme in height and complexity. However, this influence did not appear in French Canadian styles.

The earliest dress style worn in Canada was thought to be the peasant costume of seventeenth century Europe, although very few documents are available that can verify the actual dress worn by women. Men's clothing is easier to trace because it is more often visually represented in art work and described in written accounts of the time. A woman's costume seems to have been a full gathered skirt which was topped with a tight fitting sleeveless bodice. The hair would be covered with a small white cap similar to the dusting cap or mob cap popular during the nineteenth century. For outdoor or winter wear a large cape or shawl was worn wrapped around the entire figure. The man's costume included

5   These French Canadian dancing costumes represent the traditional outfits used for the lively gigue. The traditional style shirt has open neck and full sleeves. It is tied about the waist with the assomption sash.

4   Modern clothes can be adapted to portray the folk costumes of French Canadians. Dance costumes used for folk festivals are made from lightweight easy-care fabrics instead of the traditional homespun.

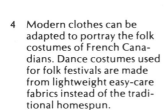

breeches, hip-length loose-fitting shirt worn over the breeches and belted with a sash, a sleeveless vest, and often a long-sleeved, hooded overcoat. The latter, known as a capot, was often worn with a sash. The sash was an extremely functional part of the costume because it could be tightened around the waist to keep in the warmth and keep out the cold winds and bugs. It was also used as a burden strap to help balance and spread the weight of heavy loads. Indian moccasins soon proved to be the best footwear for Canadian winters. Shoes and boots were expensive, often fit poorly, and were easily spoiled in the harsh Canadian climate.

The earliest immigrants brought fabrics and clothes with them, but these were soon replaced by homespun which was the most common fabric in early Canadian settlements. As soon as possible flax was cultivated and small sheep herds were tended to supply each homesteader with linen and wool. During this time, Canadians produced a unique cloth known as drugget, but most commonly called linsey-woolsey, which was a mixture of linen and wool. The cloth was used for many clothing items.

The sashes worn by the men are a unique Canadian item and have an interesting history. They are known as either assomption sashes after the town in which they were made, arrowhead sash after the design, or by the French name of ceinture flêchée. The origin of the fingerwoven sashes is now a debated subject in academic circles and perhaps no one will ever know for certain whether the Indians taught the early settlers or the early immigrants taught the Indians how to make these colorful items. Possibly the earliest French im-

Photograph courtesy of
Musée de St. Boniface Museum

6 The assomption sash is an important part of the French Canadian man's costume. It is fingerwoven in an arrowhead design and made from brightly colored wools. It is also called arrowhead or ceinture flêchée.

migrants, the nuns, taught the Indians the skill. The Indians then retained the skills after the immigrants had lost them. When interest in the early fingerweaving techniques revived late in the nineteenth and early twentieth centuries, it was the Indians who remembered them. Today, the skills involved are being taught by craft guilds and museum personnel. These colorful sashes were also woven and sold by the Hudson's Bay Company, but the loom-woven sashes were never as sturdy and durable as the fingerwoven ones had been.

Today, French Canadian dress is used by many ethnic organizations that have supported the French Canadian culture. Dance, choir, and social groups have adopted versions of the outfits worn in the early days of Canadian settlements. The fast dance known as gigue is currently the most popular dance. The usual man's dance costume consists of white shirt with full sleeves, dark trousers, often a tailored vest, and always the colorful waist sash. This is wrapped once or twice around the waist and tied at the left side. Some dance groups use a pull-on colored shirt with a pointed collar and slit opening at center front. Women's costumes show a greater variety of styles. Dance outfits usually consist of full, often tiered skirts with petticoats, white or colored blouses, bodices and/or shawls. Short puffed sleeves are common for dance blouses. A more traditional dress is illustrated in photograph 3. A long skirt covered with a spotless white apron is worn with a dark bodice, a long sleeved blouse, and a small shoulder cape. A white dusting cap completes the outfit. Cotton polyester is now the preferred fabric for making summer or indoor outfits.

In winter a capot with the traditional hood is worn at the winter folk festivals such as the Festival du Voyageur in Winnipeg or the Winter Carnival in Quebec City. The capots are still made from wool and they are often worn with corduroy trousers. Moccasin footwear is preferred.

2 Asia

China
India
Japan
Korea
Pakistan
Philippines

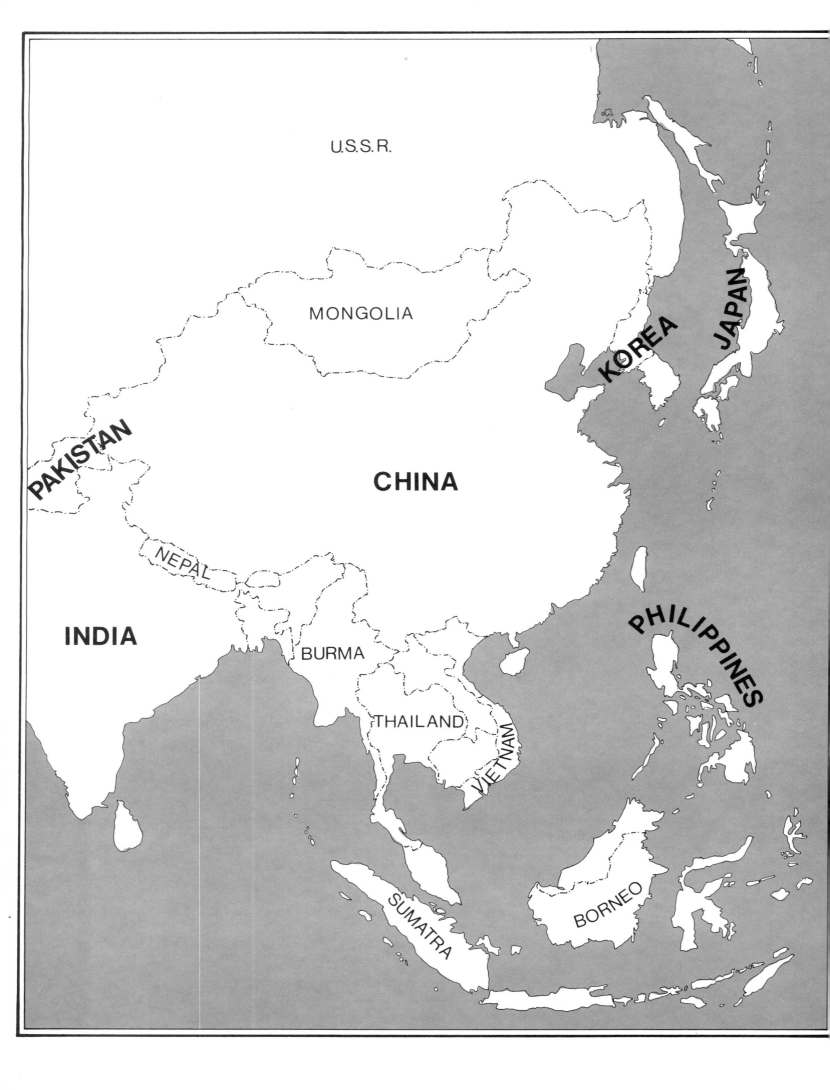

Although Asia seems a long way from Canada, a growing number of Canadian citizens have come from this part of the world. In recent years appreciation of the Canadians with Asian ethnic background is rapidly increasing. Their contribution has been noted particularly in the arts and sciences.

In Canada, Asian Canadians have come from China, Japan, India, and Pakistan. Many other peoples with Asian ethnic background live here also but they are represented in much smaller numbers. These people come from such countries as Thailand, Korea, Philippines, Burma, Malasia, and Bangladesh.

Although the total population of Canadians with Asian ethnic origin is a relatively small percentage of the Canadian total (less than two percent in 1971 census data) there has been a steady increase since World War II and a dramatic increase in immigration between 1961 and 1971. In fact, the actual numbers of people living in Canada who cite Asian origin more than doubled during this decade.

The greatest proportion of Asian immigrants have settled in British Columbia and Ontario (thirty-seven percent and thirty-five percent respectively). Sixteen percent settled in the prairie provinces, nine percent live in Quebec, and only two percent are situated in the Atlantic provinces. A further analysis of settlement patterns shows that the greatest majority of ethnic Asians live in the largest cities. Eighty-four percent live in cities of over 100,000 people, while less than five percent live in rural regions.

China

For people interested in costumes and the textiles that have been used to make them, the very mention of China brings to mind the luxurious silk fabrics that have been chosen for most of the elaborate costumes of the world. Two thousand years before Christ the Chinese people had discovered the secrets of sericulture and shortly thereafter invented the looms capable of producing exquisitely fine patterned silk fabrics.

In spite of some recent upheavals in Chinese political and social life, Chinese costume has exhibited a very slow rate of change. In part this is related to the Chinese philosophy of life which teaches respect for ancestors and tradition. Individuals must conduct their lives in such a way that no ridicule is brought to the family name. To not accept the ways of one's elders would be disrespectful. Living in accord with this way of life, the Chinese were slow to adopt new living styles and this is reflected in the dress. Change in dress did come with the revolution, but the Mao Tse-tung outfits, popular in China after 1949, are rarely seen in Canada.

Other distinctive dress styles reflect major upheavals in Chinese traditions. In Canada today we recognize a number of different costumes that are associated with the Chinese people. Most of the ethnic dress currently worn in Canada can trace its origins in the late Ching dynasty in the early twentieth century. Eighteenth- and nineteenth-century Chinese theatre and opera costumes, which have traditionally reflected the costumes of Chinese history, are also displayed in Canada.

The Chinese people are one of the oldest ethnic groups represented in Canada. The first immigrants of Chinese origin arrived from California during the Fraser Valley gold rush days of 1858. They were soon followed by immigrants from Hong Kong who left famine, poverty, and over-crowding to seek work in the Canadian mining industry. As the gold beds of the Fraser Valley were depleted, some immigrants returned home; others accepted laboring jobs in British Columbia. Those that remained were ambitious and hard working. They were willing to accept low wages and perform menial tasks. They worked in restaurants, laundries, domestic service, and at shoemaking and tailoring. Many more Chinese were brought to Canada to work on the western portion of the tracks during the building of

7 Beautiful brocaded silk fabrics and colorful embroidery are used in these costumes. This example of the twentieth-century Hong Kong sheath has matching shawl and slippers. The black skirt and shan are also typical of the Chinese outfit worn in Hong Kong. These costumes are worn in Canada only for festive occasions.

the Canadian Pacific Railway. Most of these people remained in British Columbia when the railway was completed. Some others traveled east and settled in small towns and cities across the prairies where they opened restaurants and laundries. In spite of the head tax imposed on Chinese immigrants from the early part of the twentieth century until 1923, large numbers of Chinese came to Canada. This influx came to an abrupt halt after the introduction of the Oriental Exclusion Act in 1923. Only fifty-four Chinese immigrants were admitted to Canada between 1923 and 1947. This act was repealed in 1947, and for the first time in many years resident Chinese men were allowed to bring their wives and children to Canada. Since then more women than men have been admitted to Canada and this has helped reduce the imbalance of the sex ratio.

In major urban centers in western Canada, Chinese Canadians have settled in particular areas and created "Chinatowns." The largest of these is in Vancouver; but Calgary, Edmonton, Winnipeg, Toronto, and Montreal have similar centers as well. In Vancouver during February, the Chinese New Year is celebrated with a major festival. Smaller events are held in the other Chinatowns. The harvest moon festival is celebrated in October. On both occasions street dancing and parades are common and ethnic dress is worn by many celebrants.

In the history of Chinese dress the earliest record dates from the Han dynasty (200 B.C.) which shows both men and women wearing voluminous long kimono robes that fall in soft folds around their feet. Large folds of fabric mark the sleeves and a sash is tied around the waist. This p'ao style robe, which was also the forerunner of the classical Japanese kimono, was worn until the beginning of the Ching dynasty in 1644. The Ching dynasty introduced dress restrictions to lessen the influence of previous dynasties. The Manchu conquerors introduced boots, trousers, functional riding coats, and the queue hairstyle. Although the outfits were initially functional to suit the life of horsemen from the north, the costumes were soon modified and became lavishly decorated outfits made of silk. The trousers became fuller, and often elaborately embroidered or patterned silk aprons were worn with them. The coats,

although not as full as the earlier kimonos, were magnificently adorned with the symbols of power. The mandarin collar was nearly always used on the coats and often a separate large caplike collar was attached. By the middle of the eighteenth century a dress code was established for all ranking officials. Detailed written regulations were enforced so that the rank of each official and his family could be identified by the clothing. Decoration, material, and color were specified for each garment. The general style lines of the court dress were simplified for the everyday clothing for officials and for common people. By the beginning of the twentieth century these simple, graceful garments had been accepted as the Chinese style.

The ethnic dress worn in Canada by people of Chinese ancestry originated from these nineteenth- and twentieth-century styles. The man's traditional costume still consists of silk jacket, trousers, and boots, but the excess fullness and elaborate embroidery and decoration have been eliminated. Dark colors are favored but white piping or cord is used to outline the edges of the garment and accent styling details. The jacket or shan may be worn open if it has a center front opening. In another version of the front opening the shan is buttoned diagonally from the neck, across the chest, and under the right arm. The queue has been replaced by western hair styles for men. The boots, commonly called kung fu boots because they are used for that form of the martial arts, are usually made with cloth uppers and hard soles.

Chinese ladies traditionally wear the cheongsam. In Canada this if often called the Hong Kong sheath. It is a tight fitting, sheath-like dress with mandarin collar. A slit is usually incorporated on at least one side from the hem to four to five inches above the knees. The cheongsam developed in southern China and gradually became popular in other areas. A wide variety of fabrics are possible choices for the cheongsam. Silk brocades of any color are most frequently used, but linen, cotton, and man-made fabrics are also popular. Chinese ladies wearing the cheongsam usually wear their hair in a simple chignon.

Another woman's costume closely resembles the man's outfit. Although the style illustrated in photograph 7

8 Traditional Chinese dress worn at the beginning of the twentieth century made use of luxurious silk fabrics. The man's costume is a straight jacket or shan; the woman models the cheongsam more commonly called a Hong Kong sheath.

goes back to the nineteenth century, this particular outfit is approximately fifty years old. A jacket reaching to the hip line is worn with a long pleated skirt. Traditionally the skirt would be pleated with four pleats at both sides of front and back. When the skirt is carefully pleated a front and back panel are formed, as is shown in the wedding outfit. The jacket is often embroidered with symbolic designs. The crane and tree in the design illustrated mean longevity for the wearer and the plum blossoms mean she will never have to submit to intimidation.

Festivals and weddings are important occasions within the Chinese culture and even poorer families are lavish with their resources at this time. Weddings are dazzling displays of luxurious silks, satins, embroideries, and jewels. The Chinese bridal gowns are exquisite works of art, given to the bride as a wedding gift and treasured by the family for years. Many gowns eventually find their way into museums. The bridal costume illustrated is approximately twenty years old but represents a much older style. The entire costume is covered in solid metallic thread embroidery; the bodice is of

black satin and the skirt of red satin. The bodice has four slits: at center front and back and at each side. It is closed with five frog closures at center front. The purse, known as a lucky money purse, also has a red satin base and matches the small satin slippers not visible under the beautiful outfit. The hair is adorned with a red flower and a jewel to represent the phoenix.

Jade is the gem stone preferred by most Chinese women and it is regularly used as jewelry because it is thought to bring good luck. As jade arm bands, rings, and pendants are worn the color gradually deepens and becomes more brilliant. This is considered a sign that the wearer is experiencing good fortune. Jade is now in short supply in China and must be imported from British Columbia. In China, much of the current jade jewelry is cut from Canadian stone.

Although western dress is worn by most Chinese Canadians, traditional costumes are preserved for special festivities. Dance groups specializing in traditional court dances meet regularly in many Canadian centers. The costumes worn by the young lady dancers for these occasions usually reflect Ching dynasty dress. A

9 Chinese bridal gowns may be exquisite works of art. The base fabric here is completely covered with metallic thread embroidery. Such gowns are given to the bride and worn at important functions during her married life. The gowns are family treasures.

silk jacket or shan is worn with a pair of straight cut trousers. For the ribbon dance young girls from Winnipeg wear a co-ordinated outfit of light beige silk shan and green trousers. A matching green band is used to decorate the center front and sleeve hems of the shan. Long ribbons of darker green with red fringes are held and twirled during the dance. Photograph 11 shows costumes used for traditional palace-type dancing. The red silk shan, trousers, and belt are lavishly decorated with gold embroidery. Hair would customarily be worn in a tight chignon and a glittering headdress would top the costume during a performance. All dancers wear a small brocaded or embroidered slipper and socks to match the outfit.

Although dance costumes used in Canada rarely have significant meaning, the choice of color usually reflects Chinese traditions. Red and gold represent happiness, good fortune, wealth, and prosperity. Blue and green are considered feminine colors. White has many traditions depending upon the time and location. It was usually considered the color of wealth, but in the theatre it represents the very young or the very old, and has also been used as a sign of mourning. Yellow was reserved exclusively for the emperor and his immediate family.

In Chinese theatre, opera, and ballet historical costume designs are regularly used. Not all the costumes are exact replicas of the earlier dress, but the Chinese more than any other people do attempt to portray their past dress accurately on the stage. Beautiful silk robes representing earlier elaborate styles are thus preserved. A number of dragon robes, worn in China only by emperors, court members, and nobility are now seen in Canada. Dragon robes are generally recognized around the world and are associated with the predominant dragon symbols used in the designs on the robe. The dragon robe or ch'i-fu is floor length and collarless with long sleeves and horseshoe shaped cuffs. The assymetrical closing crosses the chest, front neckline to lower right armscye and down the right side seam. There is a slit at center front from hem to about knee height for added comfort when the wearer is seated. The ch'i-fu is simple in style lines but the fabric is rich in detail and design. The twelve ancient symbols of the imperial au-

10 When performing the ribbon dance the shan and straight trousers are comfortable attire. It is especially effective when the ribbon applique repeats the design of the long ribbons.

thority are incorporated and executed in careful detail. Waves encircle the lower hem of the robe. Rugged rock mountains rise from the waves. Clouds, bats, cranes, flowers, and nine dragons are embroidered in the sky. Intertwined in the all-over designs are the ancient twelve symbols: sun disc, moon disc, constellation, mountain, dragon, flowery bird, symbol of discrimination, axe, two sacrificial cups, water weed, fire symbol, and grain. These symbols may be embroidered, woven, or painted in the five colors that correspond with the five elements, the seasons, and the directions. This elaborate and complicated use of symbolism was planned to give the magnificient robes greater cosmic significance. Symbolically and actually the wearer of this robe was thought to be the ruler of the universe. This idea was strengthened by a further belief that the robe had to be worn to be significant because the human body represented the unifying force for the entire creation.

Canadians are indeed fortunate to have access to these magnificent costumes.

11 Colorful, brightly decorated costumes are worn by Chinese dancers for the traditional palace-type dancing performances. Young people learn about their culture through ethnic dance groups who preserve traditional costumes.

India

Of all the national costumes developed in the diverse cultures of the world few are as well recognized as the Indian woman's sari. In Canada, these beautifully draped garments are only recently being replaced with western dress. Fortunately for the distinctiveness of our Canadian culture, many Indian women continue to wear the sari for festivals and special occasions. A decreasing number of women wear the sari as regular dress. On the other hand, Indian men have almost completely accepted western dress for all business and social functions. The only exception that is readily recognized in Canada is the turban headdress of the Sikh. Women in Canada who came from northern India and the area currently known as Pakistan also wear the shalwar-gamiz and gharara outfits. Some men occasionally wear the shalwar with a light loose shirt called a kurta or paharen, but more often they wear the Indian shirt with western-made trousers. Indian children of school age wear western clothing. Their cultural ties with the homeland are not as pronounced as far as the dress code is concerned.

India has one of the oldest known cultures. It can be traced back to 4000 B.C. to pre-Hindu times. The foundation of the great Hindu empire that we know today was laid between 1500 and 500 B.C. Over the centuries this culture was able to absorb and blend the traditions of many peoples who came through the northern passes of the mighty Himalaya, Hindu Kush, and Karakoram mountain ranges to settle in India. When the Muslim tradition was introduced into India, the influences of the two great religious cultures, Hindu and Muslim, co-existed and produced some of the greatest art and architecture in the world.

Indian textiles have also established a world-wide reputation that is hard to equal. Long before the time of Christ, Indian craftsmen were producing cotton textiles of finer quality than most products manufactured today on modern machines. By using only a spindle and their own hands Indian women were able to make some of the finest cotton yarns. Weavers and dyers were also part of the tradition of excellent craftsmanship. So deft were their skills that beautiful and complicated designs were produced by the precision dyeing of warp and weft

12 During the time of the
Mogul courts of the fifteenth
to nineteenth centuries,
this spectacular court dress
was developed. Even the accessories portray the wealth
of the former rulers.

yarns which were subsequently woven into fabrics with
elaborate floral and geometric patterns. The industrial
revolution in Europe and America nearly destroyed the
textile industry in India until India established its own
cotton mills early in the twentieth century to replace less
efficient cottage crafts. In recent years, however, there
has been a revival of the handmade textile-product
industry.

Garments made from finely textured, intricately wov-
en yarns have been traditional in India for costumes.
For Indian women, even those in Canada, the sari con-
tinues to be an elegant and versatile dress choice.
Photograph 13 shows an example of how the sari is
typically worn in Canada. The garment is a flat piece of
fabric usually one meter wide and between four and a
half and six meters long. The height of the woman deter-
mines the length requirement; a taller woman needs a
longer sari if it is to drape gracefully. Any lightweight,
drapable fabric can be used, but the customary Canadian
special-dress sari is made of silk. Traditionally, cotton
was accepted for the everyday or lower caste sari, but

13 The sari is one of the
most graceful and elegant
costumes of India. This example is wine silk with rich
metallic thread embroidery.
It is worn in Canada for
special occasions.

with the introduction of man-made, easy-care fabrics, nylon and polyester have also become popular. All the vibrant colors have been used for saris; black, however, is rarely worn by Hindu women as it is considered a color of ill omen.

Although the cut of the sari has not varied over the years, fashion has still been evident. Various colors, patterns, border prints, and special decorations, such as gold thread embroidery, often date the sari as accurately as fashionable skirt lengths in western dress, but few western eyes are able to distinguish these subtleties. What western fashion-conscious women have recognized is the versatility of the sari. What other garment can fit any size woman, have no zippers, hooks and eyes, or other fasteners, fold flat and fit into a small space for storage or packing, and still shake out to an elegant evening gown? The same sari can adequately hide a pregnancy or accommodate a change in weight too.

A choli, a small tight fitting blouse, is usually worn with the sari. In Canada the actual size and shape of the choli depends upon the age of the wearer and the geo-

14 A casual Indian dress is the three-piece outfit of choli (blouse), dupatta (shawl), and skirt. Embroidery has been one of the many popular decoration techniques used on Indian clothing.

graphic location of the homeland. The choli may have long, tight, set-in sleeves, round natural neckline, and be long enough to tuck into the slip. Or it may be sleeveless, have a low-cut round neckline, and reach only to the midriff. Any combination in between these extremes is possible. Traditionally, buttons are not used on a choli, but it is closed at center front with hooks and eyes or dome fasteners. This type of closure leaves a smoother front surface that won't show button bumps under the soft draped sari. The choli can be made from the same shades or of contrasting color. The fabric for the choli is often woven to the exact width.

An ankle length half-slip is worn with the sari. The slip has a drawstring waist so that it can be tied snuggly no matter what the measurement.

The sari is put on by starting at center front and wrapping one end of the lengthwise side of the sari around the waist to form a skirt. The tip of this skirt portion is tucked into the slip at the waist. Four or five large pleats are then folded into the next section of the sari and they are anchored by tucking them into the top of the slip at center front. The remainder of the sari is gradually raised and wrapped snuggly around the body once again, drawn across the bust area, and draped over the left shoulder. A married woman may wear the sari with the end drawn over her head or wrapped around once again to cover the right shoulder. A number of other possibilities for draping the sari are closely related to this basic technique. All require the Indian woman to walk sedately since no fasteners are used. Photograph 14 shows a skirt, choli, and dupatta outfit rarely worn in Canada except at cultural events, such as the Folklorama festival in Winnipeg and the Caravan in Toronto. The hand embroidery on this outfit is a beautiful example of the intricate and colorful work that is often used in India. The silver filigree jewelry is typical of the type often worn with casual cottons.

Another Indian outfit that Canadians rarely have the good fortune to see is shown in photograph 12. Today, few Indian women choose to wear the maguli because it is warmer and more cumbersome than most alternative dress. This ensemble originated in the Mogul courts during the fifteenth to nineteenth centuries. The choordor pyjamas or trousers are made from a wine colored velvet and embroidered with silver threads. The dupatta and blouse are matching silk with silver borders and trim. Small slippers are worn with this royal court outfit. They are called "shai" which translated into English means "royal." The final accent to the courtly dress is provided by a choker of pearls and rubies.

Indian women of either the Muslim or Hindu faith who accept elements of western dress usually choose pant or long skirted outfits. Legs are very rarely exposed and arms are bared only occasionally before anyone other than husband or brothers.

It is not uncommon to see Indian women in Canada wear the tika, a bright red spot on the forehead. The tika was traditonally a symbol of wifehood, but now unmarried girls occasionally adorn themselves in this way. Jewelry, too, is an important part of an Indian woman's costume. Gold and silver adornments have portrayed the family status for centuries. They are still purchased as an investment by many families.

Traditionally, Indian men also wore a draped outfit. It consisted of lungi, pagri, and ahoti or shawl, turban, and loin cloth. Although the lungi and ahoti are seen only on rare occasions, the pagri or turban is familiar in large urban centers of Canada and in localities associated with universities. Many variations of turban styles can be identified; the ingenuity, taste, and style preference of the wearer are the only limiting factors. The turban should be of a bulky, porous, and lightweight fabric so that the wearer does not suffer from heat. Usually the turban is a flat piece of cloth about thirty inches wide and up to nine feet in length. It is wound around the head at an angle, alternating from side to side, to form a ridge around the entire crown.

In Canada, most Indian men wear western business suits for formal occasions, but in casual circumstances a loose shirt, a paharen, is often worn with western styled pants. The typical hip-length paharen has long set-in sleeves, a mandarin collar, and slit opening at center front to the chest area. A band of embroidered decoration is usually placed around the collar, the center front slit, and the hems of sleeves and bodice. The paharen can be of silk, but more often it is made from soft cotton. The quality of cotton available in Canada varies from a loosely woven muslin to a soft, finely woven broadcloth.

The shalwar-gamiz and gharara outfits worn by women and the shalwar and kurta or paharen worn by men in northern India are also associated with Pakistan and I have chosen to describe these garments under that heading.

15 The pagi or turban worn by Indian men is a long piece of cloth that is wound around the head in a variety of ways. The turban is worn in Canada with western style clothes.

Japan

The graceful, elegant kimono is recognized around the world as the costume of Japan. Canadians of Japanese ancestry seldom wear this garment today; however, some examples of Japanese traditional dress are being preserved in Canada by cultural dance groups and by individuals who wear ethnic clothes for special festive occasions such as Buddha's birthday, ethnic celebrations, and folk festivals.

In Canada, citizens of Japanese origin have not always been encouraged to retain their traditional dress. From the time the first documented immigrant from Japan came to Vancouver in 1877 until after World War II the life-style of Japanese Canadians has been constantly interrupted. During the latter part of the nineteenth century large numbers of Japanese were attracted to the similar climatic and geographic conditions of the west coast. By 1908, however, strict immigration quotas limited further migration to wives and families of men already living in Canada. These groups had settled in Vancouver and the surrounding areas and this locale became the center of the Japanese ethnic community.

Although most of these immigrants arrived wearing western dress, many of the families brought their ceremonial kimono outfits with their belongings and wore them for special events in their new homes.

Western dress was not new to these people. Even before they came to Canada the widespread use of the kimono had been replaced for everyday wear by western dress styles. As early as 1872 Japanese regulations ordered the substitution of western dress for ceremonial robes because the traditional costume was so elaborate and required special care to maintain it. The regulation was later repealed, but by the beginning of the twentieth century the kimono had been largely replaced by western clothes.

After the Pearl Harbor incident in 1941 the Japanese ethnic community living along the western coast of Canada was sent to Ontario, Alberta, and the British Columbia interior. This dispersion accelerated the acculturation process, and few traditional social customs or dress habits were retained. At the conclusion of World War II many of the relocated people stayed in

16 Japanese kimonos are elegant and beautiful. Small sleeved kimonos are worn by married women. The kimonos with very long sleeves are reserved for young girls. The obi sash is tied in back with a large looped bow.

their new areas where they quickly accepted local dress styles.

Immigration of Japanese people was curtailed completely during the war and did not resume in any significant numbers until 1950. Since that time immigration has steadily increased. Today, the majority of people with Japanese ethnic origins live in the Vancouver area of British Columbia and in Ontario. Other small groups live in the three prairie provinces and Quebec. Fortunately, there is now renewed interest in Japanese cultural heritage. In Canada, attention has focused on the history of the kimono as the basis of Japanese traditional dress. Photograph 16 shows an excellent example of the woman's kimono outfit as it is worn in Canada. The outfit includes the dyed blue kimono and red and gold obi or sash, both made of silk. White tabi or socks, rice paper parasol, and an elegant hair piece known as a kansaski complete the costume.

The kimono is made entirely of rectangular pieces of fabric. The most popular choice is silk which is usually brocaded or dyed. The most beautiful kimonos are individually resist dyed after the white silk has been woven to the desired length and width. Rarely do people of Japanese origin wear the embroidered kimonos that are made in Japan for export and worn by non-Japanese as housecoats. Kimonos come in three sizes — child, youth, and adult. Extra tucks are sewn in the shoulder and waist area as needed for a proper fit. These tucks are easily removed as the person grows. The kimono is always longer than the person's height.

Another part of the kimono outfit that is essential to the costume is the obi. Today this sash is smaller and made from lighter weight, less stiff fabrics than it was in the past. Young unmarried girls often tie their obis with a large butterfly knot at the side or center back. Married women, however, are expected to wear a more formed stiffly padded double knot that often takes two people to tie correctly. A boon in recent years has been the pretied obi that can be snapped together along the edge of the bow or knot.

Married women wear the kosode or small-sleeved kimono. The long-sleeved garment, known as furisoda, is worn only by an unmarried woman.

17 The Buddhist priest and his wife are photographed with a background of cherry blossoms. The circular beads carried by the priest are used to say prayers and are similar in function to a rosary.

To achieve the look of elegance associated with traditional styles the outer kimono is worn over an under kimono that has a band around the neck opening arranged to show under the top garment. In former times many layers were worn under the kimono; today, however, most women prefer the less layered and cooler western-style underwear. The modern under kimono is held in place with a waist tie and under sash. The outer kimono, worn with the right side underneath the left, is tied just below the waist and the extra length of the kimono is folded over the waist tie and adjusted so that the kimono just covers the heels. Another waist tie and under sash are tied above the fold. Next, the obi is wrapped twice around the waist with the most beautiful part of the material appearing at center front. The ends of the obi are tightly tied at center back and the long ends are tied into a graceful knot or bow. Often a bustle pad is tied under the elaborate drum bow worn by married women to supply added support to the bow. The obijime is a narrow cord which passes through the obi bow and

18 Japanese dancers usually wear the graceful silk kimonos and obi, but occasionally specific costumes are made for special dances. For example, the tealeaf picking dance costume is a serviceable cotton and includes protection for the hands as well as an apron.

is fastened at center front in either a tight knot or with an elaborate pin or buckle. These are usually of precious metal and often encrusted with semi-precious stones. Japanese women rarely wear other jewelry. This costume is shown in photograph 17.

A Buddhist priest's robes are shown in photograph 17. The outfit consists of fuho, a black wraparound kimono, hakama, a brown full-cut trouser, and beautifully embroidered gold wagesa. The entire outfit is made from silk. On more formal or special occasions the wagesa would be more elaborate and considerably wider. In the history of costume, religious dress is often derived from earlier forms of secular dress. The hakama illustrates this tendency because it was traditionally worn by upper class women but is now worn chiefly by men as ceremonial dress.

Three girls in photograph 18 are ready for Japanese traditional dancing lessons. Traditional kimonos are worn by the girls on the right and left. Each utilizes the colorful silks and lively patterns so popular in the Orient. The center outfit portrays a version of the work outfit of a female field worker. It shows the layered cotton kimonos, obi, and red apron. Special protection for the hands are known as pekko.

Japanese footwear is also of special interest. People who traditionally wear sandals rarely wear socks as well. The Japanese thong-type sandal, however, is worn with a small cotton sock, usually about ankle height, that has been specially made with a stall for the big toe in order to accommodate the sandal strap that fits between first and second toes. Sandals are removed before entering a home or temple.

Kimonos are beautiful and graceful outfits, but Canadian Japanese women do not often wear them even in their homes or to special functions. One of the reasons for this is that kimonos are difficult to clean. Winnipeg women actually send their precious kimonos home to Japan. There they are taken apart to the original rectangular shape, washed, and carefully hand sewn before being returned to Canada.

Korea

The colorful costumes of Korea are seldom displayed in Canada. Few Canadian centers have large Korean populations, but those that do must appreciate the rich colors and graceful lines of Korean men's and women's traditional dress.

As a country, Korea was constantly subjected to the influence of more powerful neighbors. Geographically situated on the peninsula that formed the shortest land link between Japan and China, it is not surprising that the life-style of the country and its culture were shaped by outside factors. Some attempts at isolationism were made in 1636 when Korea closed her borders to all outsiders. The next two hundred years were relatively peaceful and Korean traditions were able to take root. By 1880, however, Korea's ports were again opened to international trade and by 1910 the country was completely overpowered by Japan. Even today Korean life follows two directions as a result of the partition of the country effected after World War II.

Korean dress reflects the influences of the countries that shaped its history. Although the Korean national costume is distinctive to that country, it shows particular Oriental strains in the predominance of the lively vibrant colors that can be obtained there in the natural fibers. Traditionally, cotton and hemp were the major fibers used for clothing, but silk has become more popular for festive occasions.

Koreans are noted for their love of white. In fact, they refer to themselves as "the people of white clothes." Today this is true especially for elderly men who wear white trousers or paji as an indication that they no longer are actively employed.

The women's costumes in photograph 21 show an elegant graceful outfit that consists of two main pieces. The very short bolero-type blouse is known as a chogori and the long full, high-waisted, wraparound skirt is known as a chima. The chogori is tied at center front. It has long, full sleeves which are cut narrow in the wrist area. The tie is tied in a flat bow and the long ends always fall on the right side.

The basic pattern for this chogori and chima outfit has remained virtually unchanged for centuries. It can be made from rough hemp or cotton or from rich colorful silk brocades. The same simple pattern is altered only

19 Traditional Korean dress may be made from anything from rough hemp to soft silks. Korean men and women in Canada retain their beautiful silks for special celebrations.

20   The Korean national
dress consists of a long wraparound skirt known as a
chima and a very short bodice called a chogori. The
screen in the background is
made entirely of silk with
large embroidered silk eagle
design. It was made in
Korea.

21   A handpainted silk
chogori and chima is a
priceless outfit. This one
is the first traditional outfit for this one-year-old
child sent by the baby's
grandmother in Korea.

in size. Young children also wear this graceful outfit.
The little girl in the photograph is one year old and her
costume was made and sent to her by her grandmother
in Korea.

Since the pattern for the chogori and chima outfit is
always the same, variety and individuality are achieved
by the use of elaborate textiles and lavish colors. Sometimes the two pieces are made of similar fabric, often
with border and medalion designs artistically propor-
tioned between chima and chogori. Gold and silver
threads are commonly woven into the patterns used for
the best outfits. At other times the chogori is of contrasting color to the chima. In this case the bodice of
the chogori is often white and brilliant colors are used
for the sleeves. The tie then matches either the sleeves or
the chima.

The neck edge of the chogori is always V-shaped and
bordered with a small white strip. This is outlined by a
colorful strip of fabric which usually is the same pattern
and color as the tie, but a narrower width.

Traditional male dress is illustrated in photograph
19. The costume consists of a loose jacket or chogori

with a center front button closing. Baggy, wide trousers which fit snuggly at the ankle complete this outfit. These are called paji. In recent years the traditional man's outfit has been modified: the pants are less baggy and the chogori has been reduced to a vest. Either jacket or vest is worn with the traditional white border around the V-shaped neckline.

In Canada, men have adopted the western business suit. The jacket and baggy pant outfit is reserved for at home and special gatherings. Even in Korea the business suit is the most common garb in the major cities. Only in the rural areas is the traditional dress worn.

Women in Korea and in Canada have been more inclined then men to retain the national ethnic dress. Married women and older women in particular favor the graceful lines of the chogori and chima. In Canada, however, this dress is usually reserved for festivals and home wear.

Costumes might also be worn for two important celebrations in the life of a Korean — the first and sixtieth birthdays. These occasions are always marked by family gatherings, best clothes, and a massive display of treats.

Pakistan

In recent years Canadians have become more familiar with the carefully draped and often loose fitting garments worn by Pakistani people in Canada. Since World War II, immigration from Pakistan has increased and there are now large settlements of Pakistani Canadians right across Canada. The clothing habits of Pakistani people are similar to those of India. The differences are associated with the historical background of the country and the religious traditions of Islam.

When Pakistan and India were declared independent nations on August 14, 1947, Pakistan became one of the largest Muslim nations in the world. The dress which had been typical of northern India became associated with the new country. Pakistan was further divided in the year of 1972 when east and west Pakistan separated into the countries which eventually became known as Pakistan and Bangladesh. This action further individualized the countries, and their dress styles indicate the individual preferences of the people of different nations.

In Pakistan dress habits are influenced by religious practice. Islam describes a total life-style and Muslims, the followers of Islam, look to their religious leaders for guidance in all aspects of religious, political, and cultural life. Dress, particularly for women, has been a focal issue. Although women in the earliest traditions of Islam had considerable say in society and were often freer than their counterparts in Europe at the time, their freedom gradually decreased and they assumed a more closeted home-oriented role. Various Islamic leaders, such as Qasim Amin in 1899, have argued for the emancipation of women and the relaxation of women's dress regulations. In many Muslim cultures, however, purdah, the complete covering of women, is followed, although it was not included in the original teachings of the Koran. In fact, during the annual pilgrimage to Mecca, women are forbidden the use of the veil. At the present time the Islamic world is struggling to identify a way of life appropriate to both their religious beliefs and the twentieth century.

In Canada, most women from Pakistani regions follow Islamic teaching which allows women to expose only their face, hands, and feet. Rarely do they wear clothing that exposes the body. Western dress pantsuits and long

22 The shalwar-gamiz is one of the popular Pakistani outfits that follows the Muslim dictates of covering women from neck to ankles. Pakistani women in Canada rarely wear the short dress popular in the western world.

skirts are acceptable to Pakistani women but they are not seen in dresses of street length. Sports clothing is worn modestly, but only during the actual time the women are engaged in sport.

For festivals and special occasions, Pakistani women wear their traditional dress outfits, the shalwar-gamiz or kameez, gharara, or sari ensemble. Since the sari outfit is also the outfit associated with India, I discussed it in that section. The Indian sari is worn with a shorter choli than the Pakistani sari, but otherwise the outfits are identical.

The shalwar-gamiz outfit shown in photograph 22 is often worn in Canada. It is the most practical and popular of traditional female dress. The shalwar-gamiz is a three piece outfit consisting of shalwar, gamiz, and dupatta. The dupatta is a sheer fabric scarf, just over two meters long, that is worn in a gentle V around the neck with the ends draped over the shoulders. It may also be worn draped over the head. Although the dupatta is often a solid color that matches or contrasts with the gamiz and shalwar, it can also be a beautiful border print or a tie-dyed masterpiece. The gamiz is a loose fitting, knee-length, long-sleeved tunic; however, a modified gamiz is often seen in Canada. This may be shorter, slightly more fitted, short sleeved or sleeveless, and have an enlarged neck opening. The shalwar is a pair of trousers which are gathered at the waist by a drawstring and tapered to a snug fit at the ankle. In recent years the shalwar has been less baggy than in earlier times, but it still appears to have excess length that is wrinkled around the ankle.

The fabric chosen for the shalwar-gamiz outfit depends upon the social position and wealth of the wearer. Beautiful silks are favored for special occasions in Canada, but soft cottons are also popular for cooler and less formal wear. Colors include all the vibrant intense colors associated with silks from the Orient as well as the softer more neutral colors more common in western dress.

The gharara outfit shown in photograph 23 is a bifurcated garment that creates the image of a full skirt. For more formal occasions it is worn with a short version of the gamiz or kurta and the dupatta. In keeping with its use as a formal garment, the gharara outfit is often ornately decorated with silver and gold embroidery. Although not regularly worn in Canada, the gharara is still a popular outfit to wear to a wedding. For the Pakistani bride it is made in the traditional red color which represents joy and merriment.

Jewelry is an important part of the Pakistani woman's outfit and many women living in Canada have brought their traditional jewelry from their homeland. Wealth and social position are shown by the gold, silver, and precious stones worn by the women of the extended family. Elaborate hair ornaments, earrings, necklaces, arm and ankle bands, and rings for fingers, toes, and noses are all common. The gold and silver jewelry pieces reflect the early traditions of both Greek and Persian designs which were introduced to the region around the time of Alexander the Great in 326 B.C. Today Pakistani craftsmen produce delicate filigree sterling jewelry and heavier gold pieces which are often encrusted with precious stones.

23 Although actually a very full bifurcated garment, this gharara outfit looks like a long full skirt. The gharara outfit is typical of Pakistan. It is usually reserved for special occasions in Canada.

Pakistani men in Canada usually wear western dress. For informal occasions they might wear a light loose shirt called a kurta. This is similar to the Indian paharen, but shorter. It can be made from silk, linen, or cotton and it is often decorated around the mandarin collar, neck opening, and hems with embroidery or braid. In recent years the casual loose-fitting kurta with elaborate embroidery has been introduced onto the Canadian market. It can be worn by both men and women. The embroidered designs which include flowers, birds, fruit, and leaf motifs come from the north province of Kashmir while geometric designs are produced in the other provinces.

Pakistani embroidery pieces use a rich variety of embroidery stitches. The chain stitch usually predominates, but couching, herringbone, satin, stem, buttonhole, ladder, and twisted and double cross-stitches are also common. Tunics from the desert area of Sind often feature tiny mirrors framed by the intricate embroidery patterns. The reflective power of the mirrors is greatly increased by the concave shape of each tiny disc. The sparkling shirts are attractive and popular, and are favored as casual wear by many Canadians.

Philippines

In recent years, more and more people from the Philippines are immigrating into Canada. Although both men and women have adopted western dress almost exclusively for daily wear, the Filipino national costume is worn in Canada for special occasions, folk festivals, and cultural dance group performances. Gradually, established Canadians are learning to recognize the distinctive features of the dress associated with these distant islands.

Of all the countries of Asia and the surrounding islands, the Philippines has had the closest ties with western countries. Although people living in the Philippines originally came from various areas in Asia and have the characteristics of Asian people, Filipinos have long demonstrated cultural affinities with the west. In part, this is the result of close association for they were ruled by the Spaniards for over three hundred years and were strongly influenced by the United States for another fifty years. As well, the Philippines is the only country in Asia that is predominantly Christian. Roman Catholicism was introduced by the Spaniards,

and in spite of small groups of Muslims and other local religions, Catholicism has remained the dominant religion. Like western countries the Philippines also has a good educational system that boasts a literacy rate of over seventy-two percent of the population. The country is devoted to democracy which is another feature it shares with western nations.

All of these factors have influenced Filipino dress styles with the result that no other dress style originating in Asia shows as many western traits. In spite of this the national costume exhibits a character and distinctiveness that at once identifies it. It is a blend of Asian and Western that is truly Filipino.

The unique feature that is readily recognizable in the woman's national outfit, called the terno, is the large butterfly sleeve. In no other country do sleeves have this special shape and style. The sleeve is short — two to three inches above the elbow and a little wider than a normal set-in sleeve at the hem but cut very full around the armscye seam. Many tiny pleats are used to reduce this fullness to fit the normal-sized armscye edge of the

24 The graceful baro't sayo outfit is known as the Maria Clara in the Philippines. Men wear the traditional barong tagalog which may be made from native banana fibers.

53

bodice. The result is a dramatic puff sleeve that extends almost straight upwards from the armscye, has a sharp crease along the upper edge, and then falls vertically to form a smooth side view appearance. This type of butterfly sleeve is shown in photographs 25 and 26. Butterfly sleeves maintain their rigidity in either of two ways. They can be made from material that is heavily starched or from one of the naturally stiff native fibers. Pina, a pineapple fiber and jusi, a gossamer banana fiber were traditionally used to make these sleeves and have been used to make the costumes in these photographs.

Butterfly sleeves mark the terno as distinctly Filipino; the rest of the dress, however, can and usually does look fashionable by western standards. The style lines and fabric preferences currently popular in Paris, Rome, and New York are quickly followed in the bodice and long skirt of the Filipino dress.

Another traditional woman's costume of the Philippines is shown in photograph 24. This outfit was originally known as baro't sayo, meaning skirt and blouse.

The photograph shows the traditional three piece: sayo — a floor length full skirt, camisa — a loose-fitting blouse with short set-in sleeves which have a long gather extension reaching to the wrist, and the panuelo — a shawl which is draped over the shoulders to form a high neckline at center back. Over the years the baro't sayo gradually changed from an everyday dress to a more formally decorated outfit for special occasions. In the late 1880s exquisitely embroidered, sheer camisa and panuelo were worn with a multi-paneled sayo of rich velvets and silks. This outfit became known as the "Maria Clara," a name borrowed from the heroine of a popular novel. Today the term Maria Clara is usually used to describe a less formal outfit. The sayo is rarely multi-paneled but often has a painted or printed decoration at center front and a contrasting open overskirt. The camisa has retained its original lines and decoration, but the panuelo has been extended to include a sleeveless vest that buttons at center front. The traditional embroidery and high back neckline have been maintained.

Filipino men's outfits show a greater influence from the western world. Dark slacks, just slightly fuller than a regular western cut, are worn, with a loose-fitting, untucked, light-colored shirt. The complete outfit is usually called a barong tagalog, but to be technically correct the term barong tagalog describes only the shirt. The distinctive feature of the Filipino man's shirt is the delicate embroidery, often augmented with cutout work, that adorns the center front of the garment. Although the climate of the homeland is warmer than Canada's climate, long set-in sleeves are preferred to shorter sleeve lengths in the Philippines. Until recently the barong tagalog was worn collarless, but western preferences for a collar have also influenced this aspect of the shirt. In Canada, Filipino men wear the barong tagalog for casual wear.

The fabric for the shirts is available with pre-embroidered panels, and the yardage is available in shirt lengths. A length may include embroidered pocket flaps as well as front panels. Cotton, linen, and silk are often used for Filipino clothes as well as native fabrics of pina and jusi.

More colorful outfits are used by male traditional

native dancers. Photograph 26 shows two couples enjoying the candle dance or as it is more correctly called, the dance of the glasses. The binabasohan, as the dance is called in the national language of the Philippines, is one of the most popular dances with Canadian audiences. The man's color co-ordinated costume, also known as barong tagalog, includes a print shirt with solid-colored tight fitting slacks and small neck scarf. The shirt is called a camisa de chimo, which translates to jacket of the Chinese style, and the small neck scarf has the same name as the women's scarf, the panuelo.

The women's costume for the candle dance is the traditional national dress, the terno. The girl in the green and yellow terno is also wearing the aprons common to this costume which comes from the central part of the Philippines. The tapis, or hip scarf, was usually worn knotted at the hip, and the alampay was worn over the head and shoulder. Today the size of each scarf has been reduced to a ceremonial size.

The fan dance costumes shown in photograph 27 portray yet another aspect of Filipino dress styles. The yellow silk satin camisa and brocaded skirt is an elegant princess costume worn by the Muslims in the south. The malong outfit shows oriental influence. It is a simple garment, beautifully draped, that can be worn in many ways, limited only by the imagination of the wearer. The outfit shown consists of three pieces — a scarf held in the fingers and used for movement during the dance, a printed camisa, and a malong. The malong is a remarkably flexible garment. It is a flat piece of fabric about six feet square. Two parallel edges are joined in a single seam to form a tube six feet long and about three feet wide. To wear the garment the way it is shown in the photograph, one would put the tube over the body to the under arm height. With the right hand, reach over the left shoulder and pull the excess fabric length over the shoulder. This excess fabric can then be held in the hand or tucked into the front part of the tube. This forms the graceful, almost sari-like outfit. If the weather is cold, the tube need not be bunched under the arms but can be pulled up over both shoulders and sometimes even over the head. Since most Filipino ladies are rela-

26 To perform the candle dance, or as it is more correctly called, the dance of the glasses, dancers wear the national costume of the Philippines.

tively short, the six foot length of the malong is easily wrapped around the upper part of the body for warmth. The malongs can also be used as a skirt. In this form, excess length is tucked inside the tube, and a pleat is formed at center front to adjust the width before the top of the pleat is tucked inside to hold the entire garment in place. Can you think of a more versatile costume?

The malong in photograph 27 are made from silk; however, printed cotton is often used instead. Many women choose two vertical patterns that can be draped at center front and center back.

In the Philippines the malong is usually worn by non-Christian tribes that live in the southern islands such as Jolo, Cotabato, and Lanco.

The traditional female hair styles, the chignon on either side of the head or at center back, are usually worn with Filipino dress. People around the world have grown accustomed to western hair styles for men, but women's oriental costumes still seem out of place with western hair styles. Filipino ladies often choose pale colored flowers and strings of pearls to adorn their jet black hair.

Small jewelry pieces are worn with the women's costumes. Pins set with precious and semi-precious stones are used to fasten the panuelo and malong. Early in the twentieth century, when more exposed necklines were accepted, necklaces became popular. Usually, however, the simple pendants or small neckbands are preferred to more elaborate pieces. Finger rings have long been popular with the wealthy.

27 In the south Philippines, the Muslim population have costumes quite different from the national dress. This princess costume is made from silk, satin, and brocade; the three attendants wear the versatile malong.

3 Balkan States

Croatia
Greece
Romania
Serbia

In recent years Canadians are becoming more aware of the colorful, highly decorated costumes from the Balkan States. The name Balkan was initiated during the nineteenth century and was derived from a Turkish word meaning mountainous. Since regions in this rugged area in the southeastern part of Europe have often been isolated, individual regional dress has developed. Some of the most beautiful needlework and colorful, flowing garments have originated in this area. They are now part of Canada's heritage.

The modern Balkan States include Greece, Romania, Albania, Bulgaria, and Yugoslavia. Located on one of the major landmass links between Europe, the Middle East, and the Orient, this area has always experienced foreign intervention. In recent times these countries shared a common history of five centuries of Turkish domination; yet they have developed into separate countries with great economic, religious, and political differences.

A century of turmoil within this area has triggered a major upheaval of people who left their homeland for better conditions elsewhere. Many chose North America during the twentieth century. Early migration was directed to the United States, but now a substantial number of people from this area are choosing Canada. Romanians were the first to move to Canada in significant numbers. They began to arrive late in the nineteenth century and they settled over much of Canada. In more recent times the Greeks and Yugoslavians have come. The Greek Canadian population more than doubled between 1961 and 1971. The population from Yugoslavia increased by more than fifty percent. On the other hand, Romanian Canadians are decreasing in number. This may be due to the acculturation process.

Only some of the Canadians from present-day Yugoslavia associate with the current political state. Many still refer to the former independent countries that are now republics within Yugoslavia. For that reason, Serbia and Croatia are discussed as independent states.

Croatia

In Canada, Croatian dress is regularly worn by the various Croatian Canadian cultural groups. Although the church has been instrumental in maintaining Croatian traditions, interest in ethnic heritage is now increasing and more young people are participating in choir and dance ensembles. Each Victoria Day weekend, a Croatian festival is held in some major city of Canada where Croatian Canadians meet and share their traditions. In 1979, Calgary was the host city. Winnipeg will be the location for 1980.

Most Croatians have come to Canada when political upheavals in their homeland seemed particularly discouraging and the opportunities in Canada appeared more promising. Many who came to Canada, however, left Croatia when the country was enjoying independence and so identify only with the Croatian republic and not with the larger union of Yugoslavia. Currently, Croatian Canadians have major settlements in Toronto, Windsor, and Vancouver. Smaller centers are located throughout Ontario and on the prairies.

Croatia, also known as the Hrvatska area, is now part of Yugoslavia. It includes the territory bound by the Dan-ube, Drava, and Sava rivers on the east, the Gulf of Venice on the west, Slovenia and Hungary on the north, and Serbia on the southeast. Before World War I, the area was known as part of the Austrian provinces of Dalmatia and Istria and part of the Hungarian Slavonia.

On October 29, 1918 the Croatian Diet proclaimed an independent Croatia. At that time all former ties were broken with Hungary and Austria and a union with Slavic areas was formed. This union later became known as Yugoslavia. During World War II, Yugoslavia was divided and an independent state of Croatia was again declared on April 10, 1941. A dictatorial regime lasted throughout the war, but at the conclusion of World War II, Croatia was again united with Yugoslavia. Croatia is the second largest constituent republic with thirty-two percent of the population. Although there is strength in the union of these constituent republics there is great diversity in the various cultures so joined.

Since Croatians are one of the south Slavic groups they were strongly influenced by the Roman Empire. The Byzantine Empire also affected Croatian traditions and their culture is rich in the diversity of Slavic and Balkan

28 Croatia is famous for its gorgeous embroidery and handmade Pag lace. Both are used extensively on the girl's dancing costume. White is a popular color for the man's festival outfit.

heritage. Croatian religious traditions mostly follow the Roman Catholic faith.

The dress of the country reflects the dual heritage. It is a beautiful mixture of fine lace and elaborate embroidery. Each small area of the country has its own unique detail of costume; basically, however, the woman's costume consists of embroidered blouse, skirt, and apron, while the man's costume consists of shirt, trousers, and vest.

Croatian lace from the island of Pag is world renowned. It is used extensively on ladies' garments. Ornate embroidery, similar to crewelwork has also developed into a fine art, but now machine embroidery has almost replaced the beautiful handwork of the past. Red in its various shades is the most popular color for the elaborate floral designs; but green, yellow, blue, and some orange are often included. Although many forms of regional dress are possible, one of the most popular outfits for women is from the Posacivima region. This consists of a white shirt solidly embroidered along a three or four inch vertical band at center front with embroidery completely covering the sleeves. Currently the embroidery is done by machine, but traditionally handwork was used. The pleated white skirt has an embroidered band in the back but the front is entirely covered by an apron that is all embroidery. Pag lace is used to trim the entire edge of the apron and the sleeve hems. Moccasin-like slippers are worn to complete the outfit. Traditionally, an embroidered or print kerchief would be worn wrapped around the head.

Croatian men's dress includes a hip-length white shirt, straight trousers, handwoven belt, and short black sleeveless, collarless vest. Traditionally, the trousers were white, but now dark colors are preferred. The handwoven belt is the most colorful part of the man's outfit and it is tied on top of the full untucked shirt. Since red, white, and blue represent the Croatian flag these colors may be used in belts and express strong nationalistic pride. Men's costumes are not adorned with embroidery, lace, metal buttons, or other forms of color or detail.

Western dress has now replaced these outfits for everyday wear, but the costumes are still used for festivals. In Canada they are worn by dancers who help celebrate Croatian holidays.

Greece

Greek culture has been recognized as one of the early foundations of western civilization. Its history can be traced for four thousand years. Only recently have we come to recognize the greatness of the early Minonian, Doric, and Ionian cultures that once flourished among its islands and peninsulas. In the areas of art and architecture, literature and philosophy the western world has been indebted to Greek artists and scholars. Those who have visited Greece are fascinated by the beauty of the setting and the historic importance of the ancient ruins. In more modern times the country has been troubled by invading forces and internal fighting. In Greece today there is a return of the nationalistic spirit and a drive for peace and independence.

For Greeks, immigration into Canada has been a twentieth-century phenomena. The number of Greek Canadians has greatly increased during the last twenty years. Most of them have settled in the provinces of Ontario and Quebec. Many Greeks have brought their traditional costumes with them to Canada where they are sometimes worn for special festivals. More often cos-

29 The classical Greek outfit worn for the first Olympic games is represented in a finely pleated homespun cotton. Greek costumes are collected by the Ladies Philoptorkos Society of St. Demetrios Greek Orthodox Church in Winnipeg.

tumes are worn by dance groups and members of Greek organizations for such celebrations as Oxi Day, Independence Day, or Easter or Christmas. Greek Canadians also participate in many of the Canadian folk festivals where their spritely dances are always a favorite.

In Greece, the people have been isolated from each other by physical barriers. The country is located in southeast Europe and is bordered by Albania, Yugoslavia, Bulgaria, and Turkey. Separate and distinct communities have thus arisen, even though they are often located very close to each other. Regional dress has developed in all areas.

The Greek costume reflects much of the splendor of the Byzantine Empire as well as the physical features of the country and the Greek love of beauty. Warm clothing is needed in many of the mountainous regions, waterproof clothing in the area of the sea, and lightweight clothing on the central plains. Love of color, richness of fabric, and extravagant use of metals and decoration were all used to impress the beholder and indicate the status of the wearer. Traditionally, bridal costumes were particularly elaborate, often using large precious metal buckles, belts, chains, and headdresses. Now the folk costume of Greece is rarely seen in the countryside. Ethnic dress is worn only on special occasions. The typical woman's costume now consists of a chemise, the anteri or sayias which is a type of coatdress, the sigouni that is an overcoat or jacket, a bloomer-type undergarment called braies, and a headdress. The man's costume has similar items.

The classical Greek costume portrays the time of classical Greek splendor. One can almost see the Delphi Charioteer in the white outfit illustrated in photograph 29. A similar costume was worn for the first Olympic games and has remained a popular expression of the glories of Greece. The outfit illustrated is over fifty years old and is made of homespun cotton. It has a narrow handwoven belt tied under the bust area and then crossed at center front.

The regional costume from Kastoria, the most northerly point of Greece, is illustrated in pink silk brocade. This dress was accepted early in the nineteenth century.

30 The traditional man's outfit of the Evzone warriors is now used by the Palace guard. The costume from the Isle of Crete portrays the embroidery and classical colors of the area. The long full-skirted outfit from the Peloponnisos region was made popular by the first Queen of Greece.

Although the skirt is pleated all around, more fullness is in the center back region. The cotton slip also has gathers at center back to help support the extra fullness there. The sleeveless velvet vest is lavishly trimmed with gold braid and sequins. Traditionally, the chain belt would have been solid gold, but today less expensive substitutes are used. The lace ruffles around neck edge and sleeves are homemade lace. The fez, or hat, is made of velvet with braid trim to match the vest; originally, however, felt was used for the fez. Small black shoes complete the outfit. This outfit was homemade and copied from a published pattern.

The costume worn for holidays and special events in the Phocis region has been recently copied to wear at Canadian folk festivals. In Greece, brides occasionally choose this outfit for their weddings. The long white cotton dress is trimmed with a narrow brocaded braid along the sleeve hem and top edge of the shirt ruffle. The velvet bolero is pulled on over the head and has no fastenings. It is trimmed with red and gold braid. The red apron is decorated with bands of embroidery along the lower edge. The large crepe de chine veil is trimmed with lace that matches the trim on the dress. Many gold necklace chains are worn to dramatize the outfit.

The costume from the Karpathos region is a family heirloom and is worn only for very special occasions now. The outfit illustrated in photograph 31 is over one hundred years old. It shows a costume that has been popular since the early nineteenth century. This outfit uses a long jacket that nearly covers the embroidered white dress. In fact, the dress is visible only around the neck edge and below the sleeve hems of the homespun wool jacket. The jacket is adorned with a narrow decoration along the center front opening, sleeve hems, and hem. The red satin apron is decorated with colorful ribbons and a print sash. The black wool hat is adorned with wool and silk embroidery highlighted with sequins. Black shoes and stockings complete this outfit.

The Amelia dress made popular by the first Queen of Greece was worn by town women in the Peloponnisos region. Made from silk tafetta or satin, the dress has a very full skirt and a tight-fitting bodice with a low

70

neckline. A lace dickey is worn at the neck and lace sleeves show in the large sleeves of the velvet bolero. Two slips are worn underneath to support the skirt. The short bolero is richly adorned with gold trim. In this model, photograph 30, the bolero is lined with velvet as well, but originally Queen Olga wore the bolero lined with mink. The fez has a predominant tassel often decorated with pearls and sequins and gold braid. The dress illustrated was obtained in a theatrical shop in Athens in 1964.

The costume from the Isle of Crete portrays another version of regional Greek dress which is worn in Canada for folk festivals. The white chemise and baggy pantaloons are made from homespun cotton. The white front apron is decorated with red and blue cross-stitch embroidery. The back apron or sartza is a red and blue pleated fabric that is trimmed with gold braid. As the person dances, the pleats open and the rich colors and braid are displayed. The bolero is made from wool and is hand decorated with gold embroidery. The headscarf of red and gold fringe is wrapped around the head similar to a turban. Traditionally, a woman would indicate her married status by wearing a knife in a silver sheath tucked in her red belt.

The Greek man's evzone outfit, also called foustalma, worn by the warriors from Peloponnisos, is also worn by the Greek national palace guard. Although the style is dated circa 1800, this white costume was obtained in Athens in 1940. The shirt and skirt are made of heavy cotton. The small blue woolen bolero is trimmed with silver braid, but a black bolero with gold braid is also often used. The long bolero sleeves fall freely down the back. The blue and white sash represents the colors of the Greek flag. In the past a silver belt was used to hold a weapon. White leotards are tied around the knee with garters. Red shoes with large black pompoms are worn. On the head a red fez with black tassels completes these outfits. In the blue outfit from Crete the bolero is cut closer to the neckline and a heavier fabric is used for the sash. With small exceptions these outfits worn in Canada are much the same as the traditional folk costumes in Greece.

Romania

Romanian costumes worn in Canada are nearly all imported from Romania and are among the most beautiful of all folk costumes worn here. Fine, exquisite embroidery characterizes Romanian traditional dress and makes it readily recognizable at Canadian ethnic festivals.

Most Romanians brought their outfits to Canada when they came from their homeland during the twentieth century. In Canada, Romanians settled in Hamilton, Windsor, Toronto, and Montreal in the East and in Regina, Edmonton, and Winnipeg in the West. The ornate yet dignified costume is worn at many celebrations related to the church calendar, such as Easter and Christmas as well as days for the patron saints of churches and special saint and martyr days. Seasonal festivals, such as the June twenty-fourth celebration of the seeding season and the July twentieth fair days, are still enjoyed in Romania. In Canada, Folklorama in Winnipeg, Carnival in Windsor, and Mosaic in Regina are popular celebrations for Romanian Canadians.

The country of Romania is situated on one of the major continental migration routes in southeastern Europe. Bordered by the Soviet Union, Hungary, Yugoslavia, Bulgaria, and the Black Sea, the area of Romania has been involved in most of the major migrations and upheavals of Europe. The Romanians have absorbed the life-styles and cultural influences of many nations and peoples. All this is reflected in their contemporary life patterns. In recent history the Romanians have experienced a variety of political situations. Romania was unified in the mid-nineteenth century and enjoyed independence within a monarchy from 1878 to 1947 when the Soviet Union overpowered the country. A revolt against Russian intervention was quickly stopped in 1956. Even though Romania is now allied with the Soviet Union, the people of Romania have maintained many of their cultural traditions and ways of life. In spite of collective farming and a planned economy, Romanians have kept Budapest as one of the most lively of Communist controlled cities. Tourism has been encouraged and Romanians have consistently participated in international fairs and exhibitions. Besides geographical attractions such as the Black Sea summer resorts and the winter resorts in the mountains, tourists visit the ancient monasteries and churches often dating from the fourteenth century. Folk customs and folklore, especially that of the Carpathian Mountain region, have also attracted international attention.

In Romania today, cultural events are still very popular and are supported by the government. Even in remote regions, theatre, opera, folk and classical music, and song and dance groups perform. Since the tourist industry began, renewed interest has been expressed in many of the traditional Romanian folk crafts. Wood carvings, pottery, woven carpets, Easter eggs, and glass painting have all been popular as well as the elaborate embroidered and woven folk costume.

Each region of Romania is known for its distinctive folk dress. Some areas are identified by their use of floral or geometric designs. The outfit in photograph 33 shows the costume from the Bukovina region. The wool wraparound skirt, known as a catrinţa, is almost entirely covered with metallic thread embroidery. Usually the embroidery is multicolored, but occasionally, as shown on the right, it can be a single color. The white blouse, camaşe, is decorated with many bands of red and black embroidery. Although cotton was the traditional fabric for the camaşe, nylon has proved to be an easy-care modern fabric. The camaşe and catrinţa are worn with a stiff wool, handwoven belt, commonly known as either a chinga or brau. Usually small black shoes would be worn with the outfit. With the exception of the camaşe on the left, which is over fifty years old, the other pieces of the outfits were made in the seventies.

The man's outfit from Bukovina is made of an off-white fabric and the shirt is heavily embroidered in bands around the lower edge, wrists, shoulder area, and neck edge. A heavy wool sleeveless vest is tied at the front neckline with tasseled cords. Over the shirt the gaily colored chinga or brau is tied. The chinga makes a bright contrast with the dramatic black and white color scheme. Bukovina outfits are still worn for festive occasions, weddings, and church congresses in both Romania and Canada. In Romania, the costume is also worn on Sundays. A very similar man's outfit is still worn in the

32 The embroidery from the Bukovina region is world renowned for its dramatic image and precise workmanship. Woven belts are an interesting complement for the fine work.

fields today, but it is about eighty years since the woman's costume was worn as everyday wear.

A more colorful woman's costume from Voloca in the province of Moldavia is still frequently worn in Romania. Both the white cotton blouse and wool wraparound skirt are decorated with multicolored beadwork embroidery. Beads of varying sizes are used to make the floral patterns — a more beautiful decoration would be hard to find. The blouse is below knee length and the dainty yellow embroidery shows below the skirt as well as around the sleeve hem and square neckline. The chinga completes the outfit.

In photograph 34 the blouse and vest from the Oltenia region are worn with the wraparound catrinţa from Bukovina. The cotton peasant blouse bears a simple geometric, hand-embroidered design. A black cord is used as a drawstring at the circular neckline. The velvet vest shows a relatively new Romanian design dating from the mid-sixties. Sequins and beads adorn the outside edges of the short vest.

The black and white outfit from Gorj county in the

34 The dramatic black and white outfit from the Oltenia region and the elegant white and gold costume from Banat are recent purchases from Romania. The background wall hanging is needlepoint.

76

province of Oltenia was recently obtained in Romania. The blouse is a fine white cotton with strips of black embroidery and black lace crochet around the sleeves. The white cotton skirt has very small knife pleats and a narrow band of gold trim. Although the illustrated vest is black brocade, a more typical vest would be made from wool. The sorţ consists of a front and back panel worn apron-style over the skirt. The sorţ, usually of a dark color, is decorated with cut work and embroidery and a crocheted lower edge.

The woman's costume from Banat county makes extensive use of gold and silver threads. The blouse and skirt are both made from nylon voile, but cotton would have been the traditional fabric. An elaborate floral design in gold and silver threads decorates the sleeves, scattered sections of the bodice, and hem edge. A short sorţ of velvet is heavily adorned with more gold embroidery. A crinoline and slip are both worn to support the skirt. This outfit was obtained in Romania in the mid-seventies and is worn in Canada for both Romanian and Canadian celebrations.

Serbia

In Canada, the Serbian costume is worn by Serbian Canadians for cultural events and special celebrations. An increasing interest in ethnic heritage is now being shown by third generation Canadians of Serbian descent, and they are taking an active role in ethnic organizations. The Serbian Orthodox Church has been influential in maintaining the Serbian culture in Canada and the United States where the See is established at St. Sava's Serbian Monastery in Libertyville, Illinois.

Most Serbs came to North America late in the nineteenth century. In Canada the main settlement is in Ontario. Each year on June thirtieth and July first Serbian Canadians meet at Niagara Falls, Ontario for their major festival of the year. Serbia is now part of the Republic of Yugoslavia and it is bounded by the other republics within Yugoslavia. With so many close neighbors, Serbia has had contact with an interesting variety of cultures and traditions which have influenced its own development. Serbs belong to the south Slavic peoples who came under the influence of the Byzantine Empire; they are strong adherents to the Eastern Orthodox Church.

Over the years Serbia has struggled to be an independent country. It was granted complete independence from the Turks after the Russo-Turkish war of 1877-78. In 1918, Serbia was influential in establishing an alliance comprising Serbs, Croats, Slovenes, and other smaller groups to form a kingdom which eventually became known as Yugoslavia in 1929. Although the kingdom was split during World War II, it was reunited in 1945. Now, Serbia is the largest republic in Yugoslavia with forty percent of the population.

The Serbian costume reflects the influence of the Byzantine East which is seen in the beautiful embroidery work and elaborate detail of the dress. The national costume from the area of Sumadija is illustrated in photograph 35. The woman's outfit includes a long shirt which may act as both blouse and petticoat. The blouse may have cotton crochet or lace around the hem and sometimes around the collar. It is embroidered with either geometric or floral designs at center front and upper sleeve area. Sometimes embroidery is included along the lower edge of the sleeve and along the

hem of the petticoat portion. The latter is nearly always embroidered if it is meant to show below the skirt. In many regions of Serbia, the blouse sleeve is gathered at or above the elbow and a sleeve ribbon is often worn at the gathers. Over the shirt petticoat, a long woven skirt is worn. It is usually some dark, intense color and may be decorated along the lower edge with either a woven design, sewn on bands of braid, or embroidery. The skirt is covered with a decorated apron. Some aprons show delicate embroidery work while others feature intricate weaving skills, but all are elaborately ornamented. Over the shirt a small sleeveless jacket is worn. Some jackets are the size of a small bolero and are known as kelek, others reach almost to the knees and are known as zubun. Each is decorated with elaborate embroidery. The legs are covered with knitted embroidered knee-socks; small leather slippers with turned-up toes are worn on the feet. A colorful belt is wrapped around the waist.

The Serbian woman's costume is noted for its rich embroidery work. Geometric lines are preferred but

35 Serbian outfits portray quality fabrics, rich ornamentation, and artful designs. The moccasins are styled with turned-up toes and are worn by men and women as part of the national costume.

when floral designs are used they are given straight edges to promote a linear look. One of the most popular floral emblems is the peony flower. Tradition states that red peonies grow from the blood of the Serbian soldiers who were killed fighting the Turks around the area of Kosov. The red tones in the embroidery symbolize the blood shed by the soldiers and the dark surrounding colors represent the nation's sorrow. Red, green, blue, yellow, and black are colors most often used; however, this wide range of colors is rarely used in a single design.

The Serbian man's costume is less colorful and not as decorative. A sparkling white shirt, often with embroidery along the collar, front opening, and cuffs, is worn with a small black sleeveless and collarless jacket. Trousers are tucked into the embroidered knee high socks and moccasin-like slippers with turned-up toes are worn laced to the feet and ankles. A wide woven belt adds the only dash of color to the costume.

A variety of headgear may be worn with both men's and women's outfits. Married women traditionally covered their hair with some form of scarf. In the south of Serbia, many women added coins and bangles along the edge of the scarf. Men, too, often covered their heads. One choice was a cap resembling a Canadian winter wool toque. Other Serbs wore traditional western hats or a stiffly shaped small upright hat without a brim.

In many areas of Serbia, women wear heavy necklaces which often include numerous old coins and a large variety of beads. Triangles of small beads and tassels are often joined to form a bangle. In other parts of Serbia beads are worked into the wool embroidery, and beads are often used at the ends of wool tassels as well.

Many Serbs in Canada have brought their national costumes with them and they continue to wear them here in their original form.

4 Baltic States

Estonia
Latvia
Lithuania

FINLAND

ESTONIA

RUSSIAN
S.F.S.R.

LATVIA

LITHUANIA

RUSSIAN
S.F.S.R.

BYELORUSSIAN S.S.R.

POLAND

Canadians are more aware of the Baltic States because of recent politicial history than because of their beautiful woven fabrics and folk costumes that come from that area. Not all Baltic peoples had access to the international trade of coveted dyes and fabrics; therefore, costumes developed differently in each locale. What is the same is the quality of workmanship found in wool and linen fabrics. Examples of their fine folk art are now seen regularly in Canada.

Today, the Baltic States consist of the region on the eastern shores of the Baltic Sea. There are now three republics within the Soviet Union: Estonia, Latvia, and Lithuania. Although close in proximity, they have not shared a common history. The Estonian people likely migrated to this area as early as the third millennium B.C. They are part of the Finno-Ugric peoples. The Latvian and Lithuanian peoples belong to the Indo-European language group and arrived in the area much later. Each has struggled for independence and been successful for short periods of time during the twentieth century; however, each has been mostly under foreign domination. Before and after each change of hands, large numbers of Baltic people have chosen or been forced to leave their homelands. Many chose North America. Those that arrived in Canada early in the twentieth century settled in the West; later immigrants remained near the industrial centers in the East. Toronto and the surrounding region has attracted the greatest concentration of these new Canadians.

Estonia

Estonian folk costumes have been seen in Canada more frequently since World War II when thousands of Estonians fled their homeland to make a new life in Canada. Before that time there were small Estonian settlements on the prairies around Edmonton and Winnipeg. These were made up of people who came to Canada at the time of the Russian revolution in 1917. Now the majority of Estonian Canadians live in the Toronto area where ten thousand are settled. They have language and Sunday schools and social organizations which sponsor choirs, dance groups, and social clubs. A much smaller contingency live in Montreal and they also have active organizations. Through these groups the costumes of the homeland are perpetuated.

The history of Estonians can be traced to prehistoric times. The people of Estonia belong to the Finno-Ugric family of peoples and share similarities with Scandinavians in both culture and life-styles. The area of Estonia has been hotly contested in the past century because both Germany and Russia have had interest in the territory. In fact, Estonia has existed as an independent country only when both Russian and Germany have been weak, as after World War I. Mass migration out of the country occurred after this time as Estonia experienced one foreign intervention after another.

Today, the Estonian Soviet Socialist Republic is one of the fifteen Republics in the Soviet Union. Estonia is bordered by Latvia and Russia, the Baltic Sea, Lake Peipus, and the Narva River. Although small in size and relatively sparsely populated, Estonia has developed mainly an industrial economy, but agriculture still makes a significant contribution.

Folk costumes in Estonia are similar to those worn in other Scandinavian or northeastern European countries. In Estonia there is a different costume for each region. The basic nature of the costume is the same and consists of a full skirt and matched bodice worn with a white blouse and some form of head covering. Knit stockings match the colorful handwoven belt. Homespun wool is the traditional material for skirt and bodice, but in recent years linen has been used for summer wear. The wool or linen in the skirt and bodice is arranged in

vertical stripes for most provincial dress outfits. A few regions use horizontal stripes along the lower edge. The bodice is often trimmed along the front edge with dark colors such as navy which is a popular accent. The linen shirt is always hand embroidered in white and trimmed with white lace. Very full puffed sleeves are common. The headdress is usually some stiffly underlined, upright creation that has the fabric almost completely covered with hand embroidery. Married and single women were distinguished by their headpieces. The entire costume is quietly dignified, although gaiety and enthusiasm are reflected in the hand embroidery and colorful belts.

Estonian men's dress traditionally includes a homespun linen shirt, wool knee breeches and jacket, and knit socks which are tied with colorful wool braid. The northern Estonian costume owned by the Folk Culture Centre in Ottawa shows intricate detail and workmanship. The homespun natural linen shirt has embroidery of the same color at center front, around cuffs and collar, and along the shoulder seam. A wool tie at center front

36 The beautiful fabrics
    that have made the Balkans
    famous are portrayed in this
    outfit made as the wearer's
    wedding dress thirty years
    ago. The outfit is still worn
    and enjoyed for festive occa-
    sions.

closes the neck opening. The unlined navy blue jacket is trimmed with a narrow red braid along the cut away front and mandarin collar. Nine brass buttons trim the open edge of the jacket. There are two pocket flaps at the waistline but no pockets are found underneath the flaps. The navy blue wool knee breeches have a drop front which is closed with three brass buttons. The outfit is worn with woolen socks that cover the knees. The socks are held up with a braid of multicolored wool which is wrapped twice around the knee and then tied in a windsor knot with the ends allowed to hang down the outside of the leg.

In Canada today, Estonian Canadians wear their traditional outfits for ethnic festivals. Those who came after World War II often have a special attachment to their costume. Many of the immigrants had their regional dress made for their wedding outfits. The illustrated outfit portraying the costume from the island of Mustjala was made for the wearer's wedding dress thirty years ago. The woolen fabric was ordered from the Montreal area where an Estonian lady reproduced the fabrics from her homeland. The silver ornaments on the bodice and ball buttons on the blouse or sõlg, were ordered from Sweden, where other Estonian crafts could also be obtained. The outfit was then entirely hand sewn in Winnipeg. The slippers are a recent addition to the costume. They were obtained in 1978 in Estonia. The costume is still worn today for festivals and special holidays.

Estonian choirs and dance groups in Canada use a stylized version of costumes from different Estonian regions for their performances.

Latvia

In Canada, Latvian ethnic costumes are worn by many cultural groups who preserve Latvian traditions through music and dance performances during festivals and special celebrations.

Latvian people came to Canada at the end of the nineteenth century. The largest group came after World War II, many coming directly from Sweden or the other countries to which they had fled immediately after the war.

Latvia became an independent country in 1920 after years of turmoil. Her independent spirit and nationalistic aspirations had maintained a Latvian identity through years of being overrun by foreign people, most often the Poles and Russians. In 1940, Latvia was proclaimed the Latvian Soviet Socialist Republic and has since become the most heavily industrialized republic in the Soviet Union.

Latvians or Letts can trace their origin to the Latgals who lived in the same area before the ninth century. They speak one of the two surviving Baltic languages. About sixty-eight percent of the population is Lutheran and about twenty-six percent is Roman Catholic. The population is devoted to amateur arts. Choirs, drama groups, orchestras, and dance companies are popular. Every five years, a national song festival is held in the park in the capital city of Riga and each town and local district holds its own festival and sends its best to represent the area in the national contest. In this way the national arts are kept alive and spirited.

Latvian folk costumes show great diversity among the various regions. Each small locality has distinctive dress features that have been carefully maintained over the years. The costumes share common elements with the costumes of neighboring countries, but the effects are different. The costumes are made entirely from hand-woven fabrics that have been carefully dyed with natural dyes. As in many other areas that had a limited supply of natural dyes, special value was placed on those that were hard to obtain. The red and purple dyes were especially treasured and were more readily available in the regions that had access to the sea and sea-faring trade routes. An interesting story lies behind the colors of the nica and bãrta costumes. Nica which is on the sea could obtain red dye through trade and used it for its regional dress. So that Bãrta could not copy the colors of the nica costume the Bãrta region was supplied with only enough red dye to make the women's vests and crowns but not enough to dye the entire skirt. To this day the bãrta costume has limited use of red. The outfit has scarlet vest and black skirt with a red embroidered border. The vest is trimmed with a silver braid along the edges and along the front princess line seams. The white linen blouse is embroidered with black cross-stitch along the neck edge and collar, shoulder seam and armscye, and along the waist edge. Large silver pins close the vest and blouse. Amber jewelry is worn. The red crown worn with the bãrta costume is heavily beaded and is identical to the crown worn in Nica. This crown is unique and no other Latvian crown is even similar in design.

The alsunga costume with its long purple skirt shows that this region had access to the coveted purple dye. The dark jacket with three-quarter length sleeves is decorated with red and yellow braid at center front hem and small round neckline. The linen blouse has a cross-stitched embroidered standing collar. The crown band is of shiny brass.

The zemgale costume makes use of warm earth tones. The handwoven pleated wool skirt has small gold designs woven into the horizontal stripes. The unadorned rust vest is closed with silver buttons. The white blouse is traditionally embroidered with white threads and drawn work. Embroidered socks would originally have been worn with small leather slippers known as pastalas. The crown, silver pin, and amber necklace complete the costume.

The rucaza costume is dark blue and trimmed with ribbon applique. The narrow crown to this outfit is embroidered and has ribbons that hang down the back. The hip length jacket is trimmed with red along the armscye and underarm seams. Along the V-shaped front opening a checked design of red and silver runs between the waistline and neck edge. The full skirt is trimmed along the hem with red, silver, and green bands. The white linen blouse is embroidered with red

along the collar edge, upper arm, and wrist frill. Silver and amber jewelry complete the outfit.

In the Latgale-Skilbeno district the woman's outfit includes a large cream-colored fringed wool shawl that is delicately embroidered with the same colors as the handwoven belt. Both pick up the predominant colors of the plaid skirt.

Men's costumes show the same rich variety as the women's outfits. One of the most dramatic is the outfit from Nica. A white wool jacket is adorned with black embroidery along the wrist, standing collar, V-shaped opening, center front to waistline, and pocket flaps. A curvilinear design is combined with straight lines to make an elegant pattern on the creamy white ground. The hip length jacket is well tailored and has a slight flare skirt which overlaps at center front. The unadorned trousers are tucked into the high black boots. Spangles of silver hang from top edge of the boots. The white shirt is embroidered with white thread and drawn work. It is closed with a silver clasp at the neck edge. A long red and white woven and beaded belt is tied

Lithuania

around the waist under the jacket, but the long ends hang below the jacket.

A more typical color for men's costumes is a medium grey. Often a handwoven necktie, similar to the belt, is tied in a bow that rests under the embroidered collar of the shirt.

Latvian folk dress is the treasured possession of many Latvian Canadians.

38　The white wool and black decoration of the man's costume from Nica makes a dramatic outfit; but more typical of Latvian dress are the equally well tailored grey costumes from other regions.

In spite of their relatively small numbers in Canada, Lithuanian Canadians have been active in preserving their cultural traditions. Most of these activities are supported through their church. However, choirs, theatrical groups, and dance groups are also popular in many parts of Canada, and in the Toronto area in particular. These groups wear traditional costumes and foster interest in Lithuanian Canadian activities.

Lithuanians were among the earliest immigrants into this country. Records as early as 1812 mention Lithuanians in Canada. These immigrants were usually men released from the various armed forces serving in North America. A large Lithuanian immigration to Canada started in the early twentieth century. The first family groups are believed to have come to the Sidney mine area of Nova Scotia in 1906 although these people often came indirectly to Canada. After the revolution in Russia in 1905, greater numbers responded to the chance of freer political conditions and the hope of economic betterment. The largest immigration into Canada occurred between the years 1951-61 when Lithuanian

Canadians nearly doubled in number from 16,224 to 27,629. Most early immigrants were farmers who settled in Ontario and on the prairies. Those who came later chose urban centers and got employment in industry in Montreal, Toronto, Hamilton, London, Winnipeg, and Vancouver.

The Lithuanian Soviet Socialist Republic is situated on the southeastern shores of the Baltic Sea. It is bordered by Poland, Russia, and Latvia. Lithuanians belong to the Baltic group of peoples and have established a long history of nationalistic feelings in spite of their various struggles with Russia and Poland. At the end of World War I, after years of Russian domination, Lituania was established as an independent country with the support of the Allies. Independence was recognized in 1920. The country was able to survive until just prior to World War II when Germany agreed to let Russia have domain over the Baltic States. At this time many Germans and some political leaders fled the country or were deported. Germany overpowered the Lithuanians in 1941, but in the fall of 1944, the Germans retreated and again many Lithuanians fled the country rather than accept Soviet domination. A Communist regime was set up and the Republic of Lithuania was formed. Because of the mass emigration and deportation over these troubled years, it is now estimated that 800,000 Lithuanians live outside the Baltic area. Most have settled in Sweden, the United States, Canada, and Australia.

Folk costumes from Lithuania have the same basic components as the folk costumes of other Baltic republics. Women's costumes consist of blouse, skirt, apron, vest, sash, headdress, beads, pins, shawl, handkerchief, headsquare, gloves, stockings, shoes, and winter outer garments. The complete man's outfit consisted of shirt, trousers, vest, sash, necktie, gloves, stockings, footgear, headgear, and short and long coats. Differences in costume details existed among each region of the country. Folk costumes were worn until the beginning of the twentieth century. Like their Baltic neighbors, Lithuanians used embroidery and handwoven fabrics in their garments; they differed, however, in their love of more subtle colors. Most of the original designs were geometric in nature.

The costume from the lowland region exhibited ver-

39 Handwoven fabrics, cross-stitch embroidery, and finger-woven sashes are typical attributes of Lithuanian dress. These costumes were made in Lithuar and are worn at festivals in the Toronto area.

tical stripes on the women's skirts and aprons. Costumes from the highlands were more likely to use horizontally woven patterns for the skirt and apron. All the hand-woven, vegetable-dyed fabrics have an intricate striped design, but those used in the women's outfits are considerably more detailed than those used in the men's outfits. Only the men's sashes and ties were decorated with an elaborate woven design. Both men and women wear white linen shirts that are embroidered or woven with monochromatic bands along the lower edge of the sleeves. Women's blouses often have embroidery along the collar edge and center opening as well. The vest worn by women is sleeveless and has a round neckline and a center front opening. Women's vests from all regions extend below the waist: some have a princess line and extend four to six inches below the natural waistline, others have a waistline seam and have small tabs attached to form a skirt. The vests with the tab skirts are reminiscent of the doublets worn during the sixteenth and seventeenth centuries. This outfit was usually accessorized with amber beads and brooches. A small crown was worn on the head.

The fabrics used in the men's costumes were usually chosen in solid colors of greys, browns, greens, yellows, and blues. If stripes were included they were often darker shades of the same color. Men's vests were often fitted at the waist and about six inches longer than the waistline.

The costume illustrated is waist length and has a simple border and geometric design at center front. The trousers are ankle length and have bands of decoration at lower calf height. This outfit would have been traditionally worn with knit socks, decorated at the top with an elaborate pattern, and small, flat-heeled moccasin-like slippers.

5 British Isles

Ireland
Scotland

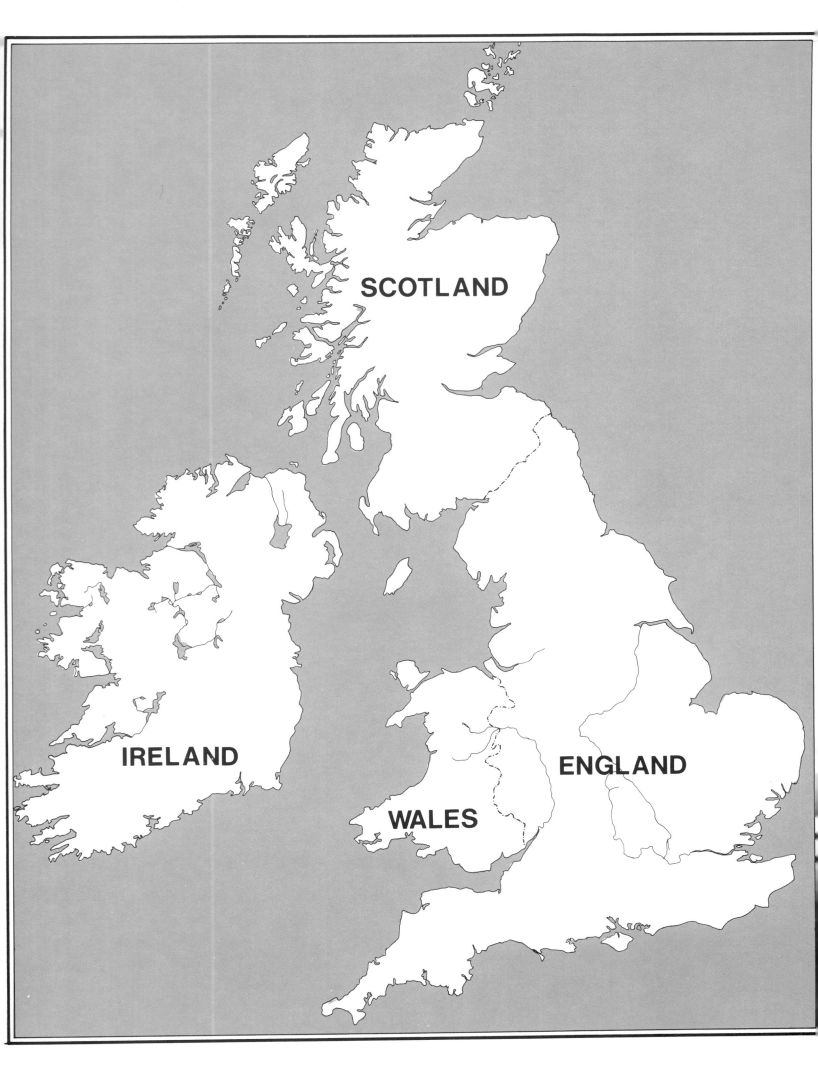

What would Canadian culture be like without the eerie drone of the bagpipes or the lively highland dances? Scottish and Irish Canadians have been so much a part of our Canadian heritage it is difficult to imagine them not being here. Everyone recognizes the kilt and plaids, and many appreciate the warm fisherman knit sweaters with their intricate patterns. Also valued in Canada are the woven woolen fabrics and fine quality Celtic jewelry that comes here from the British Isles. Even a little bit of green worn on St. Patrick's Day is a symbol of part of a Canadian's heritage.

British subjects who have come here have had a tremendous effect on Canadian culture. An unfair distinction has been made, for the purpose of organizing this book, between England and the other areas of the British Isles. Under the heading of "Founding Cultures" the general contribution of the British Isles and England in particular have been considered. In this section, the specific contribution of Scottish and Irish peoples will be discussed.

The Scottish, Irish, and Welsh people have each maintained a distinct cultural identity in spite of the long political union of Scotland, Wales, and Northern Ireland with England. Each country has even preserved some aspects of national dress even though the union occurred prior to the development of the specific folk costume we associate with those regions. Although folk costumes from Wales were not photographed for this book, Welsh immigrants have also made a significant contribution to Canadian culture.

In Canada, Scottish and Irish Canadians have settled throughout the land. Although there are major Scottish groups in the Maritimes and many Irish Catholics living in the Montreal and Toronto areas it is an overgeneralization to characterize these as ethnic settlements. People with Scottish background form the third largest ethnic group in Canada; they are closely followed by the Irish, as the fourth largest group. Both groups showed a decline in numbers between 1961 and 1971. They now live in every area of Canada.

Ireland

Irish Canadians are the fourth largest ethnic group in Canada, preceded only by English, French, and Scottish. Irish Canadians live in all major centres across the country where their traditions of dance and sport competitions are being maintained. The Irish cultural heritage is further enhanced through such ethnic festivals as Caravan in Toronto, Folklorama in Winnipeg, and many St. Patrick's Day celebrations. A great variety of folk costumes, which may range from the plaid kilt used for highland dancing, to elaborate peasant dress, to casual fisherman peasant outfits, are regularly worn at all festivals.

Irish immigration in Canada, other parts of Britain, and the United States has occurred at a high rate. In fact, it is estimated that one third of people Irish born live outside their native land. Where most western European countries have nearly doubled their populations since the mid-nineteenth century, Ireland's population in 1970 was little more than half what it was in 1841. Irish people emigrate from the Republic of Ireland, also known as Èire, which occupies just over three quarters of the Island of Ireland and from Northern Ireland at the northeast corner of the Island which has remained part of the United Kingdom. In the Republic nearly ninety-five percent of the people are Roman Catholic.

The land itself is known for its picturesque beauty, coastal mountains, rushing rivers, lazy streams, and gently rolling lowlands.

In recent years a mounting concern has been raised about the gradual disappearance of the various aspects of the traditional national culture in the homeland. The Irish language had been declining in use until it was reintroduced to the school system in 1922. Today, other cultural aspects are being promoted and preserved by such associations as the Gaelic Athletic Association, the Gaelic League, and others. Festivals are regularly held where story telling, dancing, music, and singing competitions revive interest in the historical and cultural past. In Ireland, many of these festivals now attract a large following, especially among young people. Some of the more popular festivals include Rose of Tralee, Royal Dublin Horse Show, Falway Oyster Festival, Puc

Fada Festival, and Feis Cheoil.

Renewed interest has also been shown in Irish folk costume which was similar in many ways to the dress worn by other western European countries. The women wore full skirts, puffed sleeve blouses, and vests laced in center front. The man's costume consisted of breeches, vest, and white shirt. This costume showed few details that would distinguish it from other neighboring counties.

On the other hand, fishermen and peasants near the coastal regions did develop a costume that was uniquely Irish. Even today, Ireland is famous for the arran sweaters and hats made by hand in Arran off the west coast of Ireland. This type of sweater, which can be either a pullover with V or turtle neck or a cardigan, has proved to be a warm and durable garment for fishermen. Intricate patterns are incorporated within the design, often with vertical rows of several patterns. The sweater, shown in photograph 40, is traditionally worn without a shirt, but now many people find the wool uncomfortable and prefer to wear a white shirt under the

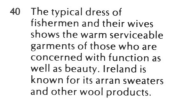
40 The typical dress of fishermen and their wives shows the warm serviceable garments of those who are concerned with function as well as beauty. Ireland is known for its arran sweaters and other wool products.

sweater. The slacks worn with the arran sweater are made from Irish tweed. Broigins or leather boots are nearly always worn as well.

The kilt outfits for dancing are similar to the Scottish kilt outfits. In fact, it was immigrants from Ireland who introduced the very early versions of the plaid to Scotland. This outfit was known as a leine. Early references are to a linen shirt that ended a little above the knees. These descriptions refer to it as light colored, but likely the color was a pale yellow because the English refer to it as "saffron shirt." Over the leine a multicolored, light wool fabric was worn. This outfit eventually developed into the kilt. Today, the kilt is worn with a white shirt, knee socks, and a croiss or waistband.

The illustrated woman's costume shows the peasant style dress. The white cotton polyester blouse has long full sleeves and small collar. Historically the blouse and slip would have been combined into a long chemise, but current preference favors two separate garments. The slip is decorated with a hem frill that shows below the skirt. This red skirt is made from a polyester gabardine, but traditionally the skirt would have been made from wool. The skirt is ankle length, A-line, and has no extra fullness at the waist. The black half apron is tied in a bow at center back. Laced up black boots would normally be worn with this outfit but convenience often dictates a small black shoe. A triangular-shaped black wool shawl with a long fringe completes the outfit.

Scotland

Scottish dress in Canada is identical to the outfits being worn in Scotland. This is because the many Scottish people who came to Canada over the years maintained association with the homeland and were able to obtain information about the highland dress as it was being worn there. The kilt is as familiar now in Canada as it is in Scotland.

In Canada, Scottish Canadians are the third largest ethnic group; they have had a longer association with Canada than any other European ethnic group. As early as 1010 Thorfinn Karlsevni sent two Scots to explore Vineland and Scots came on both French and English ship crews to participate in the early exploration of Canada. During the eighteenth century Scotland began to have a more significant affect upon the new colony when settlements were established in Nova Scotia. Substantial numbers of Scottish immigrants helped man the colony late in the eighteenth century and have continued to settle in Canada since that time. The influx of Scots can be traced to the upheavals experienced in Scotland. The English had gained control over the area and

41 The aboyne costume was traditionally worn by the female Scottish highland dancer. The pleated, checked, taffeta skirt and velvet vest are worn here with lace blouse and dancing slippers.

after local uprisings in 1715 and 1745 the English showed determination to eliminate the clan system of Scotland. At approximately the same time, the industrial revolution was beginning to affect the social structure. Peasants were being forced off their farm lands as large sheep flocks were being introduced to the highlands. Many Scots moved to urban centers for employment in the new mills, but many more chose to leave the country.

In Canada, early Scottish settlements were in the Maritime provinces, especially in eastern Nova Scotia, which still has a large Scottish Canadian population. In 1812 Lord Selkirk, after unsuccessful tries in the Maritimes and Ontario, supported the first settlement in the west at Red River. Other Scottish people involved in exploring the fur trade settled in small areas in the West. Today, there are over one and three quarter million Scottish Canadians who are living in all segments and all areas of Canada. In the western provinces there are few areas that can be identified as predominantly Scottish, but most communities have some Scottish residents who carry on many of the Scottish traditions. Highland

dancing and bagpipes are seen at social clubs, festivals, and Saint Andrew's Day celebrations across the country. During the summer, highland dancing and piping competitions and highland games are held from May through August from British Columbia to Prince Edward Island. Scottish Canadians have more ethnic folk festivals than any other group.

Distinctive Scottish dress is a recognized part of each folk festival. The tartan plaids have had a long recorded history. Plaids were initially introduced from Ireland in the mid-sixth century when the Scots moved their Celtic kingdom to the highlands of Scotland. At this time, the Scots apparently wore a linen tunic and a light wool covering of many colors. This basic costume without shoes or stockings continued until the seventeenth century when the shirt was replaced with a larger plaid. The plaid grew in size until it was five feet wide and between twelve and fifteen feet long. This could be pleated around the waist in many folds and still have fabric to drape over the shoulder or pull over the head. In many ways the plaid at this time resembled an Indian sari. The plaid would be belted at the waist and a short pouch would be worn at center front.

The date when the first tartans were produced is lost in history. By the eighteenth century the plaids were woven into the standardized elaborate tartans that we know today. Vegetable and natural dyes were used exclusively and the women who had the skill would develop very specific sets that were followed precisely. Although we now associate the tartans with family names, originally it is believed the tartans represented a particular location. But because specific clans tended to be together, the tartans began to be associated with the clans. In about 1730, an Englishman working in iron smelting in the Glengarry objected to the inconvenience of the plaid being one large garment and separated the plaid. The lower part was tailored into the permanently pleated kilt and the upper portion became the little plaid. This adaptation was extensively followed. In 1746 the English forbade the wearing of the highland dress in an attempt to lessen the influence of the clan chiefs. Once the ban on wearing the tartans was

42 In Canada, women began to wear the man's kilts for dancing much earlier than they did in Scotland. Today, the kilt is acceptable dancing dress for women throughout Scotland.

43 Country dancing outfits are not always long and formal. Short dresses and shirt sleeves may be worn as well. These dancers are from the Royal Scottish Country Dance Society.

lifted in approximately 1782, renewed interest was expressed in highland dress and the current outfit was accepted.

The kilt was originally an exclusively male outfit. In the mid-twentieth century, however, women began to wear the kilt for highland dancing in Canada. Only within the last few years has the kilt been worn in Scotland by women and there are still many who believe that the aboyne costume is the only appropriate dress for women when doing highland dancing. The aboyne costume is made from a checked (not a tartan) taffeta or similar fabric. The skirt is very full and pleated all the way around. The sleeveless vest is usually of velvet and trimmed with contrasting braid along the curved front neckline and along the center front opening. Skirt tabs extend approximately four to five inches below the waist. A white blouse with long puffed sleeves is usually worn. A strip of fabric matching the skirt is pinned to one shoulder. Small leather slippers known as brogues are worn for dancing.

Now, women highland dancers are more likely to wear the man's kilt outfit as shown in the green erskine tartan illustrated in photograph 42. The blouse and vest are similar to the aboyne outfit, but the vest may extend below the waist slightly. The kilt is cut straight across the front but is finely pleated in the back. Socks match the kilt and again the brogues are worn for dancing.

The kilt worn by men is knee length and is carefully pleated to fit tightly between the hips and waist. Two small leather belts and buckles on the hipline adjust the fullness. A kilt pin is worn attached to the lower front portion of the front flap. A sporran or pouch is worn on a chain around the waist in front of the kilt. For evening wear a fur or hair sporran if prefered, but leather is acceptable for day wear. Currently a sporran of sealskin with silver clasps and three silver balls and chain tassels is fashionable.

Another part of the ensemble is a dirk belt which is a wide leather belt with a silver buckle. The belt supports the dirk. The dirk is a combination of hunting knife and small knife and fork for eating. Today, the dirk is often a family hierloom and may be a beautiful example of metal craftsmanship. The dirk and dirk belt are not regularly worn with the folk costume today.

Scottish men wear a variety of jackets over their white shirts. The highland jacket is single breasted and extends to the bottom of the pleats on the kilt. It may be decorated with silver buttons and occasionally with braid. Design details may include shoulder straps, scalloped pocket flaps, and cuffs. For formal dress occasions a lace jabot and cuffs may be worn with the outfit. Men also wear hose that reach to within a couple of inches of the knee. The hose may be of any color or plaid; often heather, oatmeal, or light fawn are chosen. The garters may show on the outside of the turned down hose. Between the stocking and the leg, tucked into the right hose, the sgian dubh or small knife is worn. Either the balmoral or glengarry bonnet may be worn with the kilt. A plaid may also be worn, but this has been increasingly neglected in recent years. The full plaid is wrapped under the right arm and pinned to the left shoulder; however, the small plaid is also acceptable and is more popular.

The man's outfit worn for Scottish country dancing is identical to the highland dancing costume, but both jackets and plaids are often discarded for comfort. The woman's costume consists of either a long or short white dress with a plaid pinned to the left shoulder. A large brooch, often with a semi-precious stone, is used. Scottish country dance outfits in Winnipeg are shown in photographs 43 and 44.

44 Scottish country dancing is rapidly increasing in popularity in Canada. Men may wear the full kilt outfit and ladies wear a white dress with a plaid pinned on one shoulder for a formal dance.

6 Eastern Europe

Czechoslovakia
Hungary
Poland
Russia
Ukraine

The sheepskin clothing of eastern Europeans was a curiosity when first seen by established Canadians. Now Canadians have learned from these newer citizens that the ornate and richly decorated coats are suited to the harsh Canadian climate. The styles are admired and copied. Appreciated also are the colorful costumes of the dance and choir groups made up from eastern European Canadians, Polish, Ukrainian, Czechoslovakian, and Russian arts and crafts including egg decorating, folk dancing, embroidery work, and ethnic foods have enriched Canadian culture.

People from eastern Europe have been coming to Canada in large numbers since the end of the nineteenth century. During the last decade of the nineteenth century the Canadian government made an effort to attract settlers to the Canadian West. A special invitation was sent to hard-working eastern Europeans who were offered free homesteads if they settled the West. In 1896, an influx of eastern Europeans arrived on the Canadian prairies and were followed by thousands more in later years. Many of these settlers came from peasant stock, but they and their families are now at home in all aspects of Canadian life. By 1971, the greatest percentage of all eastern European Canadians lived in the largest urban centers. The exception is the Ukrainians who live mainly on the prairies.

In recent years, immigration from the areas of eastern Europe has been greatly reduced in numbers. This is especially true in those areas currently under control of Communist governments.

Czechoslovakia

In Canada, Czechoslovakian Canadians maintain their traditional costumes for their own and Canadian festivals. Their folk dress is a luxurious expression of an ancient culture that developed into distinctive regional costumes. Each locale in Czechoslovakia has its own traditional fabrics and adornment. Although the basic costume consists of the usual central European pieces — a full skirt over many petticoats, white blouse, apron, and decorative hat — fine embroidery and colorful eyelet work have added to the attractiveness of these costumes.

The country of Czechoslovakia was formed in 1918 by Czecks and Slovaks from territories formerly part of the Austro-Hungarian Empire. After World War II close political and economic union with the USSR was established and the country is now known as the Czechoslovak Socialist Republic. The name "Czechoslovakia" is the result of the joining of the two former republics of Czech and Slovak and the cultural heritage of the larger country is enriched by the union. Another notable contribution has been made by the Gypsy population. They number between two and three hundred thousand people and are probably the largest Gypsy settlement in any single country.

Emigration has long reduced the population increase of the Czechoslovakian area. The people move to other areas in the Austro-Hungarian Empire or to North America. Although it is estimated that millions of people with Czechoslovakian ancestry live in America, after the second generation only minimal ties are maintained with the homeland. The rich heritage of folk culture in Czechoslovakia has come from the various smaller territories that have contributed to the Czechoslovakian nation. Bohemia, Moravia, Slovak Socialist Republic, Silesia, and Transcarpathian Oblast all brought their traditions and their folk costumes. Even today these folk costumes are occasionally worn for holiday celebrations in the mountainous part of Slovakia, southern Bohemia, and southeast Moravia.

The costume from Piestany in western Slovakia is one of the most colorful and beautiful outfits in the country. Predominantly black, yellow, and white, it is adorned with more bright yellow, red, green, and blue eyelet. The

45 The dress from the Pohorela village near Bratislava shows the ornate designs and intricate detail common to the Czechoslovakian costume.

46 Gold embroidery on a black velvet apron trimmed with lace shows a detail of the Piestany costume.

47 The primary colors are often used together for the beautiful eyelet embroidery that adorns the costumes from many regions of Czechoslovakia.

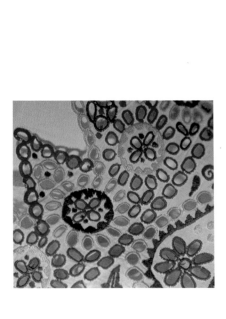

113

costume is elegant and luxurious. The fine white cotton peasant blouse has eyelet trim at cuff, full upper sleeve, and around the frilly collar. The yellow brocaded bodice is trimmed with a yellow embroidered braid and a narrow metallic braid. The full, gathered black skirt has yellow embroidery around the lower edge and a five inch lace hem. The black apron matches the skirt in fine detail of trim. This is worn with layers of petticoats each trimmed with eyelet, yellow silk satin belt, yellow ribbons tied around the lower arms, and a handmade white cap with the colorful eyelet trim along the front edge.

The man's folk costume from all regions is richly adorned. The standard outfit is white shirt, small dark-colored vest, knee breeches, and either tall dark leather boots or calf-high moccasins. Either a small pillbox type hat or a hat with medium-sized brim and crown is worn. The costume is richly embroidered or decorated with braid or large wool pompoms. The enormous pompoms are usually scarlet red and are worn around the vest, either at neck edge, on the shoulders, or at the usual position of a pocket.

In the Ruthenian region, the vest for both men's and women's outfits is often made from fur. The fur is worn on the inside with the outside of the skin decorated with colorful applique and brilliant embroidery. The men wear the vest with a peasant shirt and knee breeches; the women wear it with striped blouse and lower calf-length velvet skirt.

The outfit of Pohorela village near Bratislava, shown in photograph 45, was obtained in Czechoslovakia during the late sixties. The embroidery on the peasant blouse shows multicolored bright designs popular in that region. The red, finely pleated cotton skirt is decorated along the border with multicolored bands. Two large pleats are sewn into the apron, which is again of red cotton decorated with embroidery and ribbon applique. A bottom fringe and lace trim along the side and hem completes the apron decoration. This costume is worn for festivals and dancing in Canada, but in Pohorela it may also be worn for festivals, weddings, and baptisms.

Hungary

In Canada, Hungarian festivals are celebrated in major centers at Toronto, Hamilton, and St. Catherines. Smaller Hungarian Canadian communities in Montreal, Vancouver, Calgary, and Winnipeg also hold ethnic festivities. All make use of intricately designed ethnic costumes for dancing, displays, and holidays. Hungarian people in Canada are proud of their homeland traditions.

Hungary or the Hungarian Peoples Republic is situated in the heart of Europe and extends into the Carpathian Basin. It has a rich history closely tied to the major events of Europe's past. Hungary formed a substantial part of the Austrian Empire during the nineteenth century. After revolutions and counter revolutions the Treaty of Trianon in 1920 was signed, and large sections of the former Hungary were given independent status or were joined to other countries. Romania, Czechoslovakia, Yugoslavia, Austria, Poland, and Italy all received portions of the former Austro-Hungarian Empire. That left a small ravaged country close to its present size to try and develop a viable entity. After years of turmoil, the Communists asserted complete control and Hungary has established closer political, economic, and cultural ties with the Soviet Union.

Hungarians who were unhappy with the political situation and who were able to flee the country did leave. Over a million and a half people emigrated before the outbreak of World War II, mostly to find homes in North America. Major emigration occurred prior to the Soviet advance in 1944, in 1945, and again during the 1956 Revolution.

In spite of these social upheavals of the past century, Hungarian cultural traditions have remained firmly grounded. This area of Europe has long been recognized for its beautiful and ornate folk costumes. The people from the Kalocsa-Sarkőz region, for example, are noted for their folklore and hand-embroidered folk dress. The people of the northern plains near Mezokovesd are noted for their distinctive multicolored and hand-embroidered costumes. One of the most special garments to come from this area is the szűr, a long off-white, straight-cut coat or mantle used in the area from archaic times up to the twentieth century. Worn exclusively by men who worked in agrarian pursuits, the szűr is a warm and waterproof garment that could be used as a coat, a sleeping bag, a sandle bag, or a tent. During recent years it has been richly embroidered and appliqued. Fortunately, many excellent examples of these dramatic coats have been preserved in museums around the world.

Hungarian cultural life, rich in music and literature, was restricted to the upper classes before 1945. Since then the government has tried to bring music and particularly theatre to everyone at reasonable rates. Today, amateur groups are actively involved in preserving Hungarian traditions of poetry, carving, weaving, and embroidery. Art co-operatives sell various crafts including lace and embroidery. Major folk festivals are celebrated throughout Hungary. Some of the most popular are Rabakozi and Kisze Hajtáf, which both celebrate the end of winter and the beginning of spring. In the Paloc region, Saint Ivan's day is celebrated in midsummer. Szűret celebrates the good grape harvest in the fall.

As in other areas of Eurasia, a distinctive costume was developed in each small region. Many of these regional costumes have been brought to Canada or are made here by Hungarian Canadians. The man's costume representing the Transylvania region was recently obtained in Canada where it is worn at folk festivals. This version has a wool felt vest which is decorated with black velvet applique. The matching white wool knit breeches are appliqued with black cord. Earlier versions of these pants may have been made from soft leather. High black leather boots and a white cotton shirt complete the outfit. In contrast, the man from the Rabakozi region is wearing baggy white cotton canvas pants with a fringed bottom hem. The trousers are partially covered with a black cotton apron adorned with ribbon. A white cotton shirt with very full sleeves is topped with a sleeveless black felt vest which buttons along the center front. Normally a fur hat would be worn with this costume.

The woman's outfit from the Rabakozi region is more colorful. The white cotton blouse with peasant sleeves is covered with two beautiful shawls. The lower shawl of a fine cashmere wool and fringe is placed across the shoulders and tucked into the waist sash. A second lace shawl is worn on top of the cashmere shawl. The white

116

50 Distinctive costumes
have developed in the many
regions of Hungary. These
outfits are worn by Hungarian young people's dance
groups for such festivals
as Folklorama in Winnipeg
and Caravan in Toronto.

damask skirt is trimmed with embroidered braid
brought from Hungary. The dark apron is gaily trimmed with metallic braid.

One of the most elaborate headdresses worn in Canada
is from the Mezokovesd region of Hungary. The colorful
headpiece is worn only by married women and consists
of a colored wool kerchief with small black pompoms
sewn to it. The kerchief is wrapped around the head,
then the large multicolored wool pompoms are put on
and the entire headpiece is securely tied with string.
With this headpiece a colorful matching print skirt
trimmed with ribbons is worn. To save precious fabrics,
the center front part of the skirt covered by the apron is
a cotton insert. The apron is decorated with a wide embroidered floral band. The blouse of printed cashmere is
adorned with black embroidery at wrist and center front.

In sharp contrast to the darker colors of the Mezokovesd region, the costume from Kalocsa in the southwest
region of Hungary has bright decoration. The hat,
blouse, vest, and apron are white cotton elaborately

49 Colored wool pompoms
top a wool scarf for this
woman's headdress. The
pompoms are tied on with
string and require two people to anchor firmly.

embroidered with floral designs. The designs for the floral patterns represent the flowers grown in the region. Red poppies adorn the costume illustrated in photograph 48. They are one of the favored emblems. The skirt worn for dancing in Canada is a finely pleated cashmere with lace and ribbon trim. With the exception of the skirt, the rest of the costume was obtained in Hungary in the fifties. Occasionally in Hungary folk costumes are still used for weddings and special events. Other traditions are also followed. One of the lovely folk customs from the Kalocsa region is the pillow dance or párnaf which is performed by the bride's girl friends to show off her dowery.

The style originating in the Paloc region in the late nineteenth century is shown in a recent Canadian interpretation in photograph 50. The hand-embroidered linen apron is the only part of the costume obtained from Hungary. The cashmere skirt with lace and ribbon trim is worn with a matching fringed shawl over a full-sleeve peasant blouse. The hat is made from white satin with a stiff cotton backing. It is decorated with pearls and beads and has a large red ribbon at center back.

The outfit from the Ersekcsanadi region has a long history. It was originally worn by Turkish women and was copied by Hungarian women when the Turks invaded Hungary in the sixteenth century. The white cotton blouse has vertical black lace bands that reach to the gathering line at the elbow. Cotton eyelet sleeves also have frills below the elbow. The black sateen vest is trimmed with silver braid along center front at the waist hem. The red apron, trimmed with silver braid and black fringe, is worn over the pleated cashmere skirt. Traditionally, either wine or purple could have been used instead of red for the apron. The small hat is covered with white satin on the outside but uses black cotton on the inside. The hat is adorned with red, gold, and silver ribbon and lace. A white lace veil is wrapped over the head and under the chin. As is the custom in neighboring countries, tall boots are worn with most of these costumes. Red or black are the popular colors in Hungary, but red is usually preferred by dance groups in Canada.

Poland

Distinctive Polish dress is one of the most colorful of the folk-costume traditions now evident in Canada. Polish dress as it is worn here reflects many regions of the homeland where each town or village had its own costume. These different costumes are preserved and displayed in Canada through the activities of Polish Canadian choirs and dance groups and cultural centers. Some regional costumes are worn for formal occasions such as weddings but are rarely worn at other times.

Polish migration to Canada started as early as 1725. A slow but steady trickle of Polish immigrants, mostly refugees, continued until the 1890s when the western Canadian area was opened. Between the years 1890 and 1930 Polish immigrants, seeking better economic and social conditions than appeared available in Poland, came to Canada in increasing numbers. After World War II, immigrants continued to come to Canada but in greatly reduced numbers. This latter group consisted mostly of displaced persons who did not wish or could not return to Communist controlled Poland after the war.

Within Canada today, Polish Canadians are spread

51 Costumes from the Mazowsze region portray the rich colors possible in homespun and dyed fabrics. These dancers represent the Polish Combatants Association Dance group.

throughout the nation. Although many came to the prairies as farmers in the early twentieth century, more have settled in urban centers in Ontario and to a lesser extent in Quebec. Presently the Toronto-Hamilton area has the largest settlement with over sixty-six thousand living there. Winnipeg has the largest prairie settlement with twenty thousand. Edmonton and Vancouver each have smaller settlements.

In spite of political instability and mass migration from the country, Polish traditions have remained strong whether in Poland or transported to Canada. The nationalistic feeling of the people was the major unifying force of the country in the twentieth century. In Canada, Polish culture is sustained by church and social organizations. Traditional dances, music, food, ethnic costumes, and an understanding of the ethnic history of Poland are cultivated by these organizations.

Polish ethnic dress is also expressive of the different regions of the country. Each town or region has a distinctive costume. The dress from the south reflects the styles common to other groups from the Carpathian Mountain region: that is the sheepskin jackets, baggy pants, boots, and white homespun shirts for the men and

52 Typical dance costumes from the Krakow region show the elaborateness of Polish costumes. The man's hat is adorned with long peacock feathers.

multilayered skirts and aprons of homespun for the women. Dress from the northern regions shows similarities to Scandinavian dress and includes vest-like bodices, colorful woven, embroidered, or laced aprons, and skirts, amber necklaces, and white blouses. Costumes from northwestern regions show Germanic influences. Besides being based upon the peasant dress, Polish folk costume also has looked to the fashionable dress of the upper classes for inspiration.

The court dress of the sixteenth and seventeenth centuries is reflected in the contusze and Żywiec costumes illustrated in photograph 54. The luxurious man's contusze costume includes gold satin pants that tuck into the high topped black boots. A velvet, dark blue jacket, completely lined with gold satin, has slits for the arms and wide free-hanging sleeves. Brass buttons adorn the front of the jacket. The jacket is tied with a red and gold sash which has an elaborate fringe on the ends. The shirt may be either linen or silk satin. A silver brooch sets off the small necktie. To complete the outfit a rectangular shaped hat would be trimmed with fur. There are few

royal banquets to wear this costume to in the twentieth century; however, the contusze costume makes a spectacular outfit for dancing. The woman's Żywiec costume, from the region of the same name, is an excellent complement for the contusze costume. The pale blue skirt is covered with an overskirt of lace. The deep blue velvet vest is elegantly trimmed around the edges of the bodice and small separate sections of the tabbed bodice skirt. This bodice is a direct descendent of the doublets worn by men and women in the sixteenth century. The large white collar is reminiscent of the large ruff popular at the same time. Traditionally the collar would have stood upright, but modern fabrics are harder to starch and keep in the upright position. No doubt it is more comfortable to dance when the collar is somewhat softer. A shawl of sheer fabric trimmed with lace is worn with the outfit. Beneath the collar a bow of blue plaid fabric is worn at center front. If a girl wishes to use this costume as a bridal outfit, a hat with gold thread embroidery would complete the outfit.

More typical of the dance group costumes now worn

in Canada are the peasant outfits of the various regions. The krakowski outfit from the Krakow region is an outstanding example. The man's version is predominantly black, red, and white. The knee-length black wool sleeveless jacket is ornately decorated with red wool tassels and brass buttons. A red leather belt with at least two brass buckles is worn around the waist and supports the chains with metal discs which are worn on the right side. These jangle when the young man moves. The white shirt is decorated with white embroidery on collar and cuffs. Red and white striped cotton trousers tuck into the black boots. To complete the outfit a flat-square red hat decorated with peacock feathers and ribbon streamers is worn. The woman's krakowski costume is as elaborate as the man's outfit. Either a brightly colored print apron with white lace trim or a white apron is worn with a dark print skirt. Floral patterns are favorite prints. Gold rick-rack braid adorns the hem of the skirt. Over the white cotton blouse a small sleeveless jacket, laced at center front and decorated with embroidery, sequins, and braid is worn. Long ribbons,

traditionally attached to the floral wreath worn in the hair, are often attached to the right shoulder of the jacket for dancing. Multicolored fragile glass beads were originally worn with the costume, but because of the brittle nature of the beads, red beads are substituted now. Although red boots would traditionally indicate a married status, they are usually chosen as a dress boot for dance performances in Canada. These outfits are shown in photograph 52.

The podlazki costume is another popular dance outfit in Canada. The homespun wool used in the woman's costume is usually designed in darker colors and narrower stripes than most homespuns from the Poland regions. Deep blues, reds, and burgundies are favorite colors. The full skirts are made so the homespun is in vertical strips: horizontal applique bands are added along the hem. The apron is always of striped material but the stripes are horizontal. The black bodice is trimmed along the edge and side back seams with white, and a delicate design of red and green embroidery and gold sequins decorates the front edge. The blouse worn

54   The original man's contusze and woman's zywiec
costumes were worn to
magnificent court banquets
in the sixteenth and seventeenth centuries. Today,
these outfits are used for
dancing.

with this costume is gaily embroidered in bands along the cuff and lower arm, neck, and center front edge. A most distinctive hat completes the costume. The bonnet is made from red wool and trimmed along the lower edge with braid. At center back a floral fabric is attached and hangs down the back. The lower edge of the bonnet is trimmed with lace. The man's costume illustrated with the podlazki outfit is a very stylized outfit used by Canadian dancers to complement the lady's dress. The black jacket is trimmed with red and tied with a bright red sash. The usual puffed sleeve shirt is worn and dark slacks and black boots complete the costume.

The lowicz costume from the Mazowsze region in Poland shows the colorful homespun wool so popular in many neighboring areas. The Polish Canadian man's version of the costume illustrated in photograph 51 is made from polyester because it is lightweight and cooler to wear when dancing. The sash over the black jacket matches the trousers. The small black hat, though rarely worn, is typical of the region with its multicolored band and floral trim. The woman's costume shows the detailed hand embroidery often used on borders of the colorful striped homespun skirts and aprons. Embroidery designs include all native wild flowers from the area. Poppies and forget-me-nots are two of the most popular. This outfit is unusual because the skirt and bodice are attached and the apron is tied over the top. Pompoms usually decorate the apron ties. The black bodice is embroidered with floral designs. The blouse worn with this outfit is always hand embroidered around the cuffs, upper arm, and collar areas. A wool kerchief is tied behind the head. A typical kerchief would have floral design and fringes along the edges. Flowers are always worn in the girl's hair on her right side. Again red boots and beads complete the outfit.

There are many other Polish costumes used by dance groups and cultural associations across Canada.

Russia

In Canada, most of the various forms of Russian costume on display are worn by choir and dance groups. Some authentic traditional dress does exist but most outfits are modern stylized versions of the classical outfit which have been adapted to be more comfortable to wear and easier to maintain.

Most Russians in Canada came here before World War II. Since that time emigration from the Communist Bloc has been relatively difficult. The number of people in Canada who have indicated that Russian is their ethnic origin subsequently decreased between the 1961 and 1971 census data. There was a drop from one hundred and nineteen thousand in 1961 to sixty-four thousand in 1971. Of the urban centers in Canada, Vancouver has attracted the largest number of Russian Canadians. Toronto, Montreal, Calgary, and Edmonton, in diminishing order, also have small Russian communities. Some major cities in Canada have Russian clubs that are active in organizing cultural activities. Choirs have been one important aspect of the cultural community, but in recent years younger members have drifted away from these centers. As young Russian Canadians are assimilated into the Canadian culture they appear to have less need for the support of a cultural organization. Also many of the younger people are not familiar with the language and the Russian traditions seem remote to them.

Russia, or as it is more formally known, the Russian Soviet Federated Socialist Republic, is the largest republic in the Soviet Union. The land mass is twice the size of either China or the United States. It covers the area bordered by Norway, Finland, Poland, China, Mongolia, North Korea, and eight other republics in the Soviet Union: Estonia, Latvia, Lithuania, Belorussia, Ukraine, Georgia, Azerbaidzhan, and Kazakh. Historically Russia was the core of the expanding political entity. Many times the area was attacked by outside powers, ranging from the Mongol invasions of the Middle Ages to the Nazi devastations during World War II.

The people of this large landmass represent a great variety of cultures. In all, over sixty different cultural groups are represented, yet by far the largest percentage of the population is of Russian origin. Almost all the nationalities have deep historical roots to their areas but have established ties with neighboring localities

55 A stylized modern
version of the classical
Russian outfit is adopted
by many choir and dance
groups in Canada. The outfit is worn now only as a
costume for special folk
festivals.

in spite of their different language and life-styles.

Folk costume in Russia was thus varied from area to area. The kind of dress was largely determined by the region. There was a distinct difference between the costume of northern and southern areas while the central region showed a unique blend of both styles. The northern Russian woman's outfit consisted of sarafan, shirt, apron, and belt. The shirts were usually of linen and were elaborately embroidered at neck area, collar, sleeve, and lower hem. Often the shirt was long enough to serve as a petticoat as well as blouse. Over the shirt a sarafan, or joined bodice and skirt, was worn. During periods of prosperity, Russian women would wear sarafans made from luxurious velvets, brocades, and silks; most often, however, peasant women wore sarafans of homespun linen which were sometimes block printed with vegetable dyes. Colorful embroidered aprons often adorned the outfits. A short warm jacket with long sleeves was sometimes added.

In the south, the woman's costume was distinguished by the poneva, shirt, and apron. The shirt was richly embroidered with colorful designs. The poneva or skirt was made from three lengths of checked woolen homespun. The poneva often was not closed at center front so that part of the long shirt would show under the apron. The apron, richly adorned, usually reached to breast height and was anchored over the shoulder with narrow straps. The most spectacular part of the woman's costume was the headdress. As is common with all Slavic people, married women were expected to keep their hair covered at all times. The koloshnik headdress, although of different shapes for various areas of Russia, was usually extravagantly decorated. In the north, pearls and gold embroidery often covered the entire hat. In the south, semi-precious stones, pieces of mirror, and tinsel were also used. In the latter half of the nineteenth century, as textile manufacture became industrialized, a kerchief with a floral print largely replaced the expensive koloshnik.

Men's costumes were not so elaborate or colorful. Men wore their tunic-like shirts over the trousers. The shirts often had an assymetrical closing on one side and were made from homespun linen or from purchased cotton, silk, or wool. A great variety of belts were worn over the shirt. Trousers were baggy and often tucked into the top of high boots.

In Russia today, folk costume has almost been replaced by urban, western dress. The only people who seem to have retained their ethnic dress are the nomadic reindeer hunters and herders of the far north. One reason for this is that the reindeer outfits are the warmest and most comfortable for their work. In the northern Cau-

Ukraine

casus region urban dress has been accepted but some items and styles of the folk costume have been retained. In this area sheepskin hats, quilted jackets, silver ornate belts, and shawls are still popular.

Russian Canadian outfits are worn rarely in Canada. The outfit illustrated shows a modern version of a sarafan, made from polyester and trimmed with commercial braid. Red is and has been the most popular color for Russian costumes as it symbolizes goodness and beauty. The white shirt, unadorned in the photograph, is typical of most Russian costumes. The modified koloshnik is color co-ordinated with the outfit and trimmed with gold braid. This version is not as elaborate as the historical headdress. The necklace worn with the outfit represents individual taste. Red beads would be the traditional accessory.

In Canada today, Ukrainian Canadian young people are seeking knowledge about their ethnic heritage. They are accepting Ukrainian traditions and incorporating features of the Ukrainian heritage into their everyday lives. This has become noticeable particularly in dress, where the delicate embroidery designs of ethnic folk costumes are included on fashionable modern clothes. Nearly all major centers on the prairies have some Ukrainian organizations that are furthering Ukrainian culture and interest in Ukrainian traditional costumes. Folk festivals are common in many small and large communities. The Edmonton Ukrainian Bandurist Chorus and the Ukrainian Festival of Dauphin are now internationally known. Ukrainians are proud of their Ukrainian origin.

Immigration from the Ukraine to Canada started in the 1890s. During the period 1891 to 1914 over one hundred and eighty thousand immigrants came to Canada from the Western Ukraine. Most of these people settled in Manitoba and the areas eventually to become Alberta and Saskatchewan. Another major influx of

Ukrainian immigrants came between 1921 and 1939. Most of these immigrants were farmers, but many professionals and craftsmen came as well, looking for political, economic, and cultural freedom. After World War II a third and much smaller wave of immigrants came from the Ukraine. This group represented people who were displaced during the war or those who were trying to escape Communist domination. Today, nearly sixty percent of Ukrainian Canadians live in the prairie provinces and nearly thirty percent live in Ontario. Others live in British Columbia, Quebec, and the Maritimes. The city of Winnipeg has the largest Ukrainian Canadian population but it is closely followed by Edmonton and Toronto. Approximately one third of all Ukrainian Canadians live in rural areas.

Ukrainian settlers, especially the earliest ones, faced immense hardships on the Canadian prairies. They were handicapped by the difference between farming methods on the prairies and in the Ukraine, their lack of understanding of English, and their lack of capital. But their self-sufficient nature, their frugal living habits, and their determination helped them succeed in developing productive farming units from unbroken prairie.

The Ukraine is now known as the Ukrainian Soviet Republic. It lies in the southwest region of the European Soviet Union. Besides other regions of the Soviet Union it is bordered on the west by Hungary, Czeckoslovakia, and Poland. Since 1917, the Ukraine has been dominated by the Communist Party. According to its constitution, the Ukraine is allowed to enter into direct relations with foreign states, but in actual fact, the ties so permitted are of limited importance and most ties are with other Soviet Union regions. Nearly all the people living in the Ukraine are classified linguistically as Slavs. The highest percentage of them are Ukrainian and Russians, but small representations of many other groups exist there as well.

Ukrainian folk dress reflects much of the early history of the Ukraine area. It has incorporated features from neighboring countries and from trading partners during the Middle Ages up to the late nineteenth century. Evidence of Indian silks, Persian and Italian brocades, French velvets, Greek and Turkish ornaments and designs all found their way into Ukraine folk dress. Each region has a slightly different dress, but there are seven basic costumes that represent various areas of the Ukraine. Three costume types are from the Carpathian Mountain region: the hutsul, boyko, and lemko costumes. The polissyan costume is worn in the north and the dnieper-type costume is worn along the Dnieper central region. The pokutto-bukovinian costume is worn in the southwest region and the volhyn-podillyan costume is worn in the central section of the country. The costume of the east and central plains, the Poltava and Kiev regions of the Ukraine, developed along similar lines and gradually became recognized as the formal national dress of the Ukraine. The costumes most often seen in Canada are modified versions of the original costumes.

Ukrainian dress was a living costume in many parts of the Ukraine even at the beginning of the twentieth century. Many immigrants brought their long skirts and sheepskin jackets with them to Canada. Now, however, the outfits have been replaced by modern fashionable dress in both the Ukraine and Canada. Costumes are worn only for festivals. Two major costume types dominate the Canadian scene: the poltava-kiev outfit and the costumes of the Carpathian Mountains. I have chosen to talk about only these two costumes because of the limited space.

The traditional version of the woman's poltava-kiev outfit includes a number of distinctive basic parts. A long embroidered shirt acts as both petticoat and blouse. This shirt has a narrow band of embroidery along the lower hem and detailed, elaborate bands along the upper arm of the full sleeve. Embroidery, usually cross-stitch, is also placed along the narrow cuff, armscye seam, and narrow collar. Scattered embroidery decoration is common over the lower sleeve. Over the shirt, a wraparound skirt or plakhta of colorful woven fabric is worn. The skirt often does not meet at center front and usually has wool tassels at lower center front corners. An apron, embroidered or decorated with colorful braid, is

56 The colorful costumes
    from the Poltava Kiev area
    are usually used by dance
    and choir groups in Canada.
    These outfits are worn by
    members of the Orlan Dance
    Ensemble in Winnipeg.

57 In the Carpathian
    Mountain region many
    styles of colorful costumes
    are worn. Various Ukrain-
    ian cultural groups through-
    out Canada are preserving
    ethnic cultural heritage.

worn over the skirt. It is two to three inches shorter than the skirt, which is an inch or two shorter than the shirt, so three distinct layers are obvious at the lower portion of the outfit. A sleeveless hip length jacket is worn over all. The jacket, often made from velvet, may be decorated with braid along all the edges. A multi-strand necklace of red coral is worn with the outfit. Low heeled, high topped red boots are usually worn although black is also an acceptable color. Ukrainian women place considerable emphasis on headgear. Young girls braid ribbon and flowers into their hair and leave long streamers of ribbon to fall freely. Many times wreaths of flowers and ribbons are worn on top of the hair. Married women are usually expected to cover their hair with a scarf or to wear their hair braided and wound around the head. In fact, an important aspect of the wedding costume included the symbolic changing of hair styles and head coverings. Colors are always very carefully chosen for the national costume. The entire outfit is color coordinated. The white shirt is embroidered in predominantly red, although small accents of black, yellow, and blue are occasionally seen. The jacket and apron pick up colors from the woven skirt.

The man's poltava-kiev outfit consists of an embroidered white shirt with decoration along the narrow stand-up collar and the center front. There is a small tie at the neckline. The shirt is full in body and sleeves. Very full trousers are pleated at the waist and tucked into the top of the red boots. The trousers are usually made of a luxurious fabric such as velvet or satin. A wide woven belt or poias is wrapped a number of times around the waist and left to hang at the left side. The outfit would be completed with a full collarless jacket, just below knee length, which has baggy sleeves. A sheepskin hat with tassel may be worn as well.

Besides the poltava-kiev regional dress many extremely intricate costumes come from the Carpathian Mountain regions. Similar items are included in the dress, but the style of wearing them and the decorations are different from the eastern regions of the Ukraine. Today, costume from this area is popular because it is so colorful and distinctive. It illustrates the spirit that is truly Ukrainian. The woman's hutsul costume includes a long embroidered shirt, two woven aprons worn in front and back, woven belt, and short, straight, heavily decorated vest. The vest is usually white with black borders along all openings and with detailed embroidery which is predominantly red, but includes some yellows and greens. This garment is usually made of soft sheepskin.

In the Lemko region of the Carpathian area, women wear short blouses with skirts. An apron is worn over the skirt and both are usually made from contrasting commercial materials such as cotton. Black and dark blue are common colors. The shirt embroidery, although no less delicate than in other areas of the Ukraine, usually covers a smaller portion of the shirt sleeve. Normally, only a narrow band around the upper arm and cuff is decorated. A sleeveless short straight jacket, often dark blue or black is also worn. A similar costume for men is still popular. They wear full cut trousers that usually tuck into the top of their stockings. Colorful stockings are used by both men and women in Carpathian regions. They are knit with a colorful decorative border at the top edge. Small leather slippers, almost moccasin-like, with turned up toes are worn with cross lacings around the legs.

In Canada, the stylized Ukrainian costume has retained many of the features of the homeland dress. The poltava costume is used most often by dance and choir groups. Couples who dance together usually wear color co-ordinated outfits. That is the male and female partner will both wear the same predominant color. In groups of many couples, each couple may wear a different color or they may all have the same color scheme. Although traditional costume is seen, it is now common for women to wear a colorful print or embroidered skirt rather than a skirt and apron. The colorful poias are tied around the waist. The headdress for the young woman is often worn instead of a kerchief, the usual hair covering of married women. Men's outfits do not always include the jacket but the traditional outfit is faithfully followed in most other ways. The costumes of the mountainous Carpathian regions are usually good representations of earlier costumes, although less baggy pants and modern shoes are often substituted for the leather slippers and full cut trousers.

7 Scandinavia

Denmark
Finland
Iceland
Lapland
Norway
Sweden

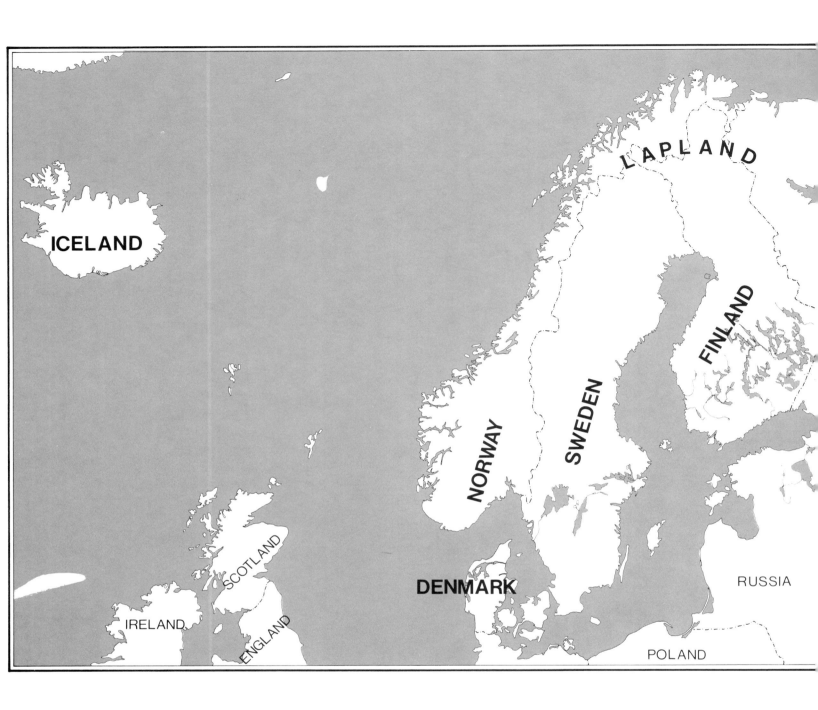

ICELAND

LAPLAND

FINLAND

NORWAY

SWEDEN

SCOTLAND

IRELAND

ENGLAND

DENMARK

RUSSIA

POLAND

Canadians have long treasured their association with fellow citizens from Scandinavia. Our inheritance from them is a variety of specialized crafts — embroidery work, beautiful wood carvings, and rosemaling, the colorful patterns used on many wooden objects.

Scandinavians, inhabiting lands of mountains, lakes, rivers, lowlands, and miles of rugged coast lines, developed regional costumes suited to each specific area. Their present keen interest in their own cultural heritage has redirected their search for regional costumes that have been lost over the years. In many cases entirely new folk costumes are being created, often from descriptions preserved in pictures and written records. Scandinavian folk costumes in Canada are either made here or brought from the homeland, some as finished garments, others as material to be made up. All of the costumes seek to preserve the dress image associated with the homeland district.

Scandinavians have been in Canada for the past one hundred years. Icelandic Canadians have a major settlement in the Interlake area of Manitoba; they have maintained very close ties with the Icelandic homeland. Finnish Canadians have a large settlement in the Lakehead. Norwegians have settled in Vancouver, Edmonton, Saskatoon, Thunder Bay, and throughout Manitoba. Eighty percent of Scandinavians settled here before World War II. As with other groups, those that came early in the twentieth century founded farms and chose the prairies and part of Ontario as well. Now fifty percent of Scandinavian Canadians live on the prairies, nearly thirty percent live in British Columbia, and the remainder are spread throughout the more eastern areas of Canada.

Denmark

Danish ethnic folk costumes are worn in Canada when Scandinavian folk festivals are held. Usually, Danes join with other Scandinavian people to celebrate special holidays and feast days. Otherwise Danes are inconspicuous in the Canadian mosaic. Those Danes who have immigrated into Canada have tended not to settle in any identifiable groups; rather Danish people have quickly blended with those of the host country.

Although Denmark is densely populated very little emigration has occurred in the last few decades. The smallest of the Scandinavian countries, Denmark is close in geographic location and cultural ties to northern Europe and the other Scandinavian countries. Denmark, in fact, has managed to be the link between the two cultures and has evolved its own culture that is influenced by both. Sharing a land border only with Germany, Denmark is almost entirely surrounded by the sea. This also has been a major factor in characterizing the Danish life-style. Because of the easy access to the sea, the Danes have long been powerful and important seafaring people. The Vikings established their reputation on the seas over a thousand years ago, and this has been continued by generations of Danish explorers and fishermen.

59 The dress from Praesto
county of Sjaelland Island
is shown as it would be
worn on weekdays. A white
apron is worn on Sundays
and special occasions.

Clothes to accommodate this way of life have been adopted by the Danes. Their folk costume is very different in character from the neighboring peoples although the basic pieces are the same. Women wear a full skirt with a white blouse, a close fitting jacket, and a shawl. Heads, especially for married women, are always covered. Long stockings and clogs or shoes cover feet and legs. As is common in all the Scandinavian countries, each small region in Denmark had its own regional dress. These traditional costumes were preserved for longer periods of time in isolated regions of the main peninsula and on the islands. However, Danes did have good ties with the rest of Europe and they were influenced by fashionable western dress before many of their neighbors.

The dress from Praesto County, Sjaelland Island is shown in photographs 58 and 59. The little girl's costume is identical to the woman's costume. This is typical of Scandinavian folk dress. A white linen blouse is worn under the cotton and wool dress. The blouse may be ankle length and act as a slip as well. The dress has metal rings at center front for lacing and yellow and green horizontal stripes bordering the hem of the full skirt. The

58 Children's clothes are miniature versions of adult dress, as is shown in this outfit from Praesto in Denmark. The costume was made by hand and was functional in Canada several years ago.

143

60   From the home region
of Hans Christian Andersen,
in Odense Fyn, comes this
delightful red dress and bonnet outfit. Some handwoven
fabrics are made on the loom
also shown in the photo-
graph.

adult version of the outfit has pleats in the skirt back. The red and green striped fabric is a popular choice in that area. The cotton apron is always white for festival or special occasions but during the week, for everyday events, a colorful print apron is chosen. A triangular scarf is always worn around the neck. The two front points are securely tucked into the front of the dress bodice. The back point is allowed to hang freely down the back of the dress. Shoes or clogs may be worn with the outfit. One of the most dramatic aspects of the costume is the bonnet. The crown portion of the adult bonnet illustrated is a family heirloom and has been carefully preserved for over one hundred and fifty years. The remainder of the bonnet has been recently remade by hand. As well as being tied under the chin, both bonnets have a bow and long streamers at the back. The child's bonnet is trimmed with white ribbon, the adult bonnet with red ribbon streamers. The bonnets are trimmed with lace along the face edge. The dresses illustrated have been homemade in Canada with materials brought from Denmark. The child's dress is thirty years old now, but is still proudly worn for festivals.

Areas of Denmark that had thriving urban centers and contact with high fashions from other countries often adopted a folk costume that more closely followed modern western dress. This is evident in the costume worn in Odense Fyn which is one of the major cities and industrial centers of Denmark and is also the birthplace of Hans Christian Andersen. Because of western influence the costume from this region is the only regional dress that has a low exposed neckline. The bright red long-sleeved wool dress is decorated with a blue ribbon appliqued along the border. Over the dress a tight fitting sleeveless vest is worn. The vest has blue ribbon trim along the edges and a little embroidery on the skirt tabs. Although the illustrated vest is made from wool, a brocade is a more traditional fabric. A checked cotton apron is gathered to a narrow waistband and is tied under the skirt tabs of the vest. A white blouse with only the neck frill showing over the dress neckline is worn underneath the dress. Either wooden clogs or leather shoes are worn. Over a white lace undercap a red and silver brocaded bonnet is tied under the chin. A large blue bow decorates the back of the bonnet. The costume illustrated in photograph 60 was made in Canada from local fabrics. Today, this costume is worn for folk festivals and dancing.

144

Finland

Finnish costumes in Canada are worn for folk festivals and special holidays. Two major Finnish events in Canada are the July first celebration and the June twenty-fourth celebration of the longest day of the year. The former is a celebration that has originated in Canada, but the latter is a festival that was brought from Finland where much of the country experiences the midnight sun. Choir and dance groups in Canada also wear a version of ethnic dress.

Because of social and economic conditions and political unrest, many Finnish people emigrated to North America late in the nineteenth century. The first immigrants settled in the northern mid-western United States where the climate and scenery were similar to their homeland. Immigration into Canada started somewhat later, but by the beginning of the twentieth century Finnish immigrants were moving into the northern areas of Ontario. The number of Finnish Canadians increased steadily until the 1930s when conditions in Canada proved less favorable than in Finland. Today, there are major Finnish settlements in Toronto, Thunder Bay, Vancouver, Sudbury, and to a much lesser extent, Montreal.

Finland is the most easterly of the Scandinavian countries and is bordered by Norway, Sweden, and the Soviet Union. Independence was declared on December 6, 1917, but this was not recognized by the Soviet Union until 1920. Since that time a large section of the Karelia region and all the Petsamo region have been turned over to the Soviet Union. The area that is now Finland is an independent republic and only fifteen percent of her trade is with the Soviet Union.

Geographically, Finland is similar to the other Scandinavian countries. Glaciers, mountains, rivers, lakes, valleys, and miles of coastline characterize the country. Because Finland is farther east it does not receive the modifying effects of the Gulf Stream. Consequently the winters are much longer and more severe. Cross-country skiing is considered the national sport, but running, water skiing, riding, hunting, and fishing are also popular. Climate and terrain have influenced activities and dress.

The history of Finnish costume has been very closely related to Swedish dress. Both have accepted the peasant country dress as their national outfit and since the two countries shared a common history for six hundred of

the last eight hundred years it is reasonable to expect similar costume. As in other areas of Scandinavia, fashionable western dress was accepted by upper class people for most of the last four hundred years. Interest by the upper class in folk costume, however, began by the 1840s. National spirit was being emphasized and a general romanticism toward local history was being expressed. Initially, upper class people used reproductions of peasant dress that they found illustrated in art works for masquerade costumes. Later, reproductions were worn on occasions where a regional or nationalistic spirit was desired. This concept of a national dress was not well received in all areas of the countryside. Elderly people remembered the folk dress as it had been worn and they viewed the "new" outfits with suspicion. Often there was a noticeable lack of authenticity. Young people, on the other hand, were proud of the costume they saw as a return to traditional dress. Each group was looking for a lasting and representative national dress, but each had different ideas how this would be accomplished.

61 The costume from the Härmä region shows the classic costume of Finland consisting of woven skirt, white blouse, tight fitting bodice, and apron. This costume was brought to Canada from Finland.

In the twentieth century, folk costume in Finland has developed along similar lines to the folk costume in other Scandinavian countries. Each district or region has a local costume. The basic parts of the woman's costume are wool skirt, bodice or vest, white blouse, small hat or ribbon hair bands, skirt bag, and possibly an apron. Red and green are the predominant colors of nearly all the Finnish national costumes. Yellow, blue, and black are regularly used as accent colors. Today, national costumes are available in Finland as ready-to-wear outfits in specialty stores. The slightly gathered skirts are woven from wool and always have some form of vertical stripes. Bodices are often made from the same fabric as the skirt, but are also popular in dark velvet. Eyelets or lacing rings are used at the center front of the bodice. Usually the lacing shows but occasionally the lacing is hidden on the inside of the bodice. The white linen blouse always has long sleeves and a small stand-up collar on a round neckline. Low heeled black shoes are preferred footwear.

Hat styles distinguish young unmarried girls from married women. Young girls wear ribbons tied around their hair and have long colorful ribbon streamers hanging down the back or side. Married women wear some form of shaped hat. White lace is one of the most popular fabrics for women's hats but other fabrics and colors are also used in different districts. Skirt bags are often of similar fabric and colors to the skirt and bodice, but occasionally intricate embroidery and applique are seen as well. Silver, brass, or gold pins or necklaces are an important part of the Finnish costume. Often the pieces worn are treasured heirlooms. As a general trend Finnish outfits on the west coast more closely resemble Swedish outfits and those on the east border show some Russian influences.

In Canada some liberties are taken with the authentic Finnish costume. Although many women send to their homeland for outfits and most choose the costumes from their home region, some prefer costumes from other regions and order these instead. Another variance is that Finnish Canadian married women often choose to wear the ribbon headdress rather than the hats officially recognized as part of their costume.

The costume from the Härmä area of Finland has a green silk apron covering most of the front of the woven wool skirt. The undecorated black velvet vest is laced at

148

Iceland

center front with a red tie. The small hat is adorned with long ribbon streamers of red, green, black, and yellow. Although cream colored cotton stockings are part of the costume they are rarely worn in Canada.

A similar costume from the Jurva district was brought to Canada eight years ago. The bodice is made from navy velvet and red, green, and blue ribbons are worn in the hair. The woven vertical design in the skirt shows some of the ornate geometric designs that are popular in handwoven fabrics in the midlands of Finland. From the Karelia district in the southeastern region a matching striped bodice and skirt are part of the regional dress. The bodice of this costume has lacing rings along the center front edges. The skirt bag popular in these areas is sewn from the major stripes in the skirt fabric. Traditionally fingerwoven narrow belts were used to hold the skirt bag. Today a fine belting is used.

The outfit modeled in photograph 63 is worn in the Vancouver area and shows the costume popular in the Laihia region of Finland. The most obvious difference between this costume and the costumes of other areas is the lack of visible front lacing on the bodice and the more elaborately decorated skirt bag.

For the last one hundred years, Canadians have had a pleasant association with Icelandic immigrants. Sigtryggur Jonasson, who came to Ontario in 1872, was the first Canadian Icelandic immigrant. He was influential in organizing more groups of immigrants who attempted to settle in Ontario and Nova Scotia. Later a permanent Icelandic area, christened "New Iceland," was chosen in the interlake region of Winnipeg in Manitoba. The first Icelandic settlement was called Gimli in 1875. The settlers organized their own republic and ran affairs in their own language until Gimli became part of the province of Manitoba in 1887. Immigration increased and other major settlements in the interlake were started as well as small settlements in other areas of the province and in areas of Saskatchewan, Alberta, and British Columbia. Today, Manitoba is proud to have the largest Icelandic settlement outside Iceland. The area includes Gimli, and Winnipeg to a lesser extent, and is considered the social and intellectual center of Icelandic culture on this continent. Gimli, in fact, is referred to as the "mother of Icelandic settlements."

Iceland itself, a republic since 1944 when independence from Denmark was gained, is a volcanic island

64   Each year, during the Icelandic festival in Gimli, a Maid of the Mountain or Fjallkonan is chosen to preside over the festivities. The picture of the Viking ship in the background was painted by the husband of the lady in the photograph.

located slightly northwest of Sweden, Denmark, and Norway. It is a country with great variations of climate. Glaciers are still active in many areas, yet warm ocean streams from the south prevent the harbors from freezing. Moderate temperatures usually prevail all year round. Because of Iceland's volcanic origins, geysers and hotsprings are common. The latter have been utilized to heat homes and public buildings. This reduces heating costs and makes Icelandic heating systems the envy of Canadians in this age of high cost fuel. Iceland is one third larger in size than Ireland but its total population is only two hundred thousand people.

In Iceland everyone is equal in a classless society. Women have always attended co-educational schools and have had the right to vote since 1918. Icelandic women rarely change their names when they marry: only when they emigrate to North America do they accept the surnames of their husbands.

Icelanders in Canada learned the new language and customs, yet maintained their native language and traditions. Their descendents have a rich Icelandic heritage which is restated each year during the Icelandic celebration, Íslendingadagurinn, in Gimli. At this time a woman who has made an outstanding contribution to the culture and the community is chosen to be the Fjallkonan and to greet visitors to the festival.

To mark these important celebrations in Canada, Icelandic women's costumes have been preserved in spite of the cost involved. However, many costumes have been altered slightly from the Icelandic originals because of the difficulty in obtaining the gold and silver jewelry and the threads for the traditional embroidery.

Men's costumes, however, have attracted little attention. Men's attire was similar to traditional western peasant dress. Either pants which were full and shapeless and tucked into the top of the boots or breeches ending just below the knee where they tied tightly were worn. The shirt was a simple, shapeless style with long sleeves and was decorated with a black ribbon tied at the collarless neckline. The jacket was also collarless and was usually unshaped. It was made of a dark wool fabric and was closed at center front with many buttons. A flat wide-brimmed felt hat completed the outfit. Today, men's costumes are rarely seen.

In Iceland three types of women's dresses are still used, the peysufőt or dress-up costume, the upphlutur or every-day costume, and the skautbűningur or festive dress. The skautbűningur is lavish, expensive, and not often used. It is reserved for important dignitaries for special occasions. The peysufőt is worn occasionally by elderly ladies for special outings. The upphlutur is most often worn and is now considered the national dress. It features a long skyrta of heavy wool serge or black velvet gathered to a narrow band at the waistline and richly embroidered with gold and silver threads in a floral design around the hem. The fitted, short vest or hufa matches the skirt and is worn tucked into the belt at the waistline. The low square front neckline and center front opening are richly embroidered in gold and silver. The vest is fastened by a gold chain which is laced across center front and fastened in a gold clasp. With the vest and skirt, a long-sleeved loose-fitting white shirt is worn. The neckline is collarless and has a short slit at center front. This opening is closed with a gold or silver, round-shaped pin. The sleeves are cuffed at the wrist. Extra fullness of the skirt is often bloused out over the low neckline of the vest. Although a fine white cotton was the traditional fabric for the blouse, other fabrics and colors are now accepted. An apron is always worn with the costume, but it was never meant to be functional. The apron is slightly gathered to a waistband and is long enough to fall a few inches below the knees. The aprons are always made from a rich fabric such as taffeta, lace, or satin and can be of any color or design — striped, checked, plaid, or plain. A gold or silver belt is worn with the costume. The belt is often sectional and some sections may be left free to hang down at center front. A small black knit toque-shaped headpiece with a long black tassel is the usual hat. The tassel end is decorated with a silver or gold ring about three inches long. Dark stockings and small soft black slippers complete the costume.

Icelandic Canadians who cannot obtain the gold and silver jewelry are resorting to simulated pieces. Even tin-

65 The national dress of Iceland is known as the upphlutur. The vest is laced with a gold chain and fastened with a large gold clasp. Other gold ornaments may also decorate this costume.

foil has been used to decorate costumes worn by choirs and dance groups. The rich embroidery is being replaced by commercial braids and similar findings. Quite often, only the parts of the garment actually seen needed to be made from the fashion fabric. The wool skirt of the Icelandic costume in the Folk Cultural Centre in Ottawa has a cotton center front which was effectively hidden by the apron. Almost all cultures from around the world have used this technique to conserve the expensive fashion fabrics of their clothes.

Another costume regularly seen in Canada during the Icelandic celebrations is worn by the Fjallkonan or Maid of the Mountain. The Fjallkonan is a personification of Iceland and was first introduced in the poem written circa 1810. The poem has since been accepted as a popular song for Iceland and is regularly sung by Icelandic Canadians at their festivals. Fjallkonan is more than a symbol of Iceland, she is the nation itself. The first visual presentation of Fjallkonan appeared in an English translation of Icelandic folktales. The Icelandic Day celebration of 1924 was the first Canadian festival to have a reigning Fjallkonan. Since then she has appeared every year to welcome home the children of Iceland.

The Maid of the Mountain has sometimes worn the skautbúningur outfit. Most often, however, her costume consists of a long white gown that is gathered gently to a yoked round neckline. It has long full sleeves and is usually decorated with two rows of gold braid trim at the hem, sleeves, and neckline. An ornate gold belt is always worn. A full length green velvet cape trimmed with ermine or other white fur is worn with the dress. The crown is the traditional headgear of the skautbúningur outfit. The headdress has three basic parts. The hip length white veil is gathered on a drawstring and tied around the base of a padded form. The veil is always white and can be made from any sheer fabric. Organza and tulle are favorites. The edge of the veil is usually trimmed with lace. If the lace is narrow it is often slightly gathered. The veil is then draped over the form. The heavily stuffed horn-shaped form is about three inches wide and shaped like the letter "C" balanced on

154

top of a base. Two long white satin ribbons are attached to the back of the form and hang freely under the veil at center back. The top of the "C" shape is now only about six inches above the head although in the past it was often at least a foot high. Around the base of the form a flexible gold cornet is fastened. The cornet may be worn on top of the veil, but is most often secured underneath. Cornets can be extremely elaborate and may have interesting leaf fillet or curvilinear designs executed in gold.

The colors of this costume represent the colors of Iceland. The white dress and veil depict the ice-covered mountains and winter landscape while the grass green cape portrays the summer scenery of Iceland.

The Fjallkonan's costume has had only minor changes in detail and decoration. Slight variations in choice of fabric and jewelry are noted from year to year, but basically the Fjallkonan has remained the unchanging, never faltering symbol of Iceland. The custom and the celebration are an annual Canadian event.

Lapland

When Canadians think of Lapland, visions of reindeer herds usually come to mind. Herding and hunting, in fact, have been central to the life of Lapps for over two thousand years. The semi-nomadic and nomadic life-styles, the northern climate, and the isolation have dictated a unique way of life and this has influenced clothing choices and styles.

Lapland is a geographic, not a political entity. It stretches across the most northern part of Europe and lies largely within the Arctic Circle. The area includes northern Norway, Sweden, Finland, and the most northwestern corner of the USSR. Because of the great differences in geographic conditions, three main types of Lapp culture have developed.

The Lapp costume is distinctive yet rarely recognized outside of Lapland. The distribution of Lapp costume has been rigidly controlled and no costumes either old or new are allowed to be taken from the country. Only a few people have been successful in taking the costumes from the area. The few costumes that are in Canada are worn in public only for special occasions.

Lapp dress is nearly always dark blue with scarlet and yellow trim. A wool cloth is used for summer wear and reindeer hide that is tanned, dehaired, and dyed is used in winter. The costume has three main pieces — a decorative hat, tunic, and breeches. The tunic, known as kapta or peski depending on the geographic location of the wearer, has long sleeves, little or no collar, and a gathered skirt. In very cold weather two tunics would be worn. As is common in the Canadian Arctic, the inner tunic would have fur next to the skin to obtain the greatest possible amount of insulation. Tunics are decorated around the neck edge and hems of sleeves and skirt with rows of yellow, red, and green bands. Young men's outfits often had so much decoration that the entire outfit was nearly covered. A sash or leather belt is worn over the tunic. This belt is used to hold the pukko (a form of hunting knife). Men from the northwestern areas also wore a lariat of braided deerskin over one shoulder and under the other arm.

The man's traditional hat — the hat of the four winds or sorcerer's cap — had four large stuffed points that were

worn pointed in each of four directions for the married men or all pointed forward for the single man. This versatile hat had three points stuffed with eiderdown while the fourth point was used as a purse. Similar use of headgear is reflected in the Canadian eastern Arctic where pouch-type hats are used as purses. More recently in Lapland single pointed or peak hats have become common. Knitted band-type hats are also worn and are adorned with colorful bands of decoration and a tassel of long strips of brilliantly dyed reindeer hide. Young boys often decorate their hats with vividly colored wool pompoms. The outfit was completed with red socks (over the leggings) and pointed reindeer shoes known as mutåkas. The toes of the mutåkas gently curl upwards.

The woman's costume is very similar to the man's version. The dark blue wool tunic with slightly longer skirt is heavily decorated with red and yellow bands. The woman, too, wears the pointed toe mutåkas which traditionally were stuffed with sedge grass for extra warmth. Red socks, breeches, and braided thong belt to support the pukko are also part of the outfit. The female hat is smaller and less dramatic than the man's headgear. In-

66 The Lapp costume is restricted in use to the northern area of Scandinavia. This child's costume features the blue color that is favored in Lapland.

Norway

stead of points, the woman's hat is shaped like a small pillbox with two short lappets hanging down each side back.

The Lapp outfit shown in photograph 66 is a modern version of the traditional dress. It is an authentic outfit that was made and smuggled out of Lapland approximately ten years ago and it is worn here by a young Canadian girl. Although the sash is worn around the neck in Canada it would likely have been worn wrapped around the waist in Lapland. The sash ends may have been as low as the ankles. The decoration on this costume follows the traditional color scheme but the bands are much narrower and less dramatic than earlier dress. There is a red plastron or dickey at center front that is surrounded by gold-thread embroidered good luck symbols. This outfit does not have the waistline seam that was common on earlier outfits.

The mutăkas of reindeer hide and fur are sized to fit the foot snuggly without any additional liners. The pointed toes are gently curled upwards and held there by the expertly cut design. This outfit does not include breeches and the traditional red socks.

Canadians picture Norway as the home of the bold and exploring Vikings who were the first Europeans in recorded history to visit the shores of North America. This colorful and dramatic ancestry is reflected in the Norwegian folk costumes worn in Canada by Norwegian Canadians who are interested in preserving their cultural heritage.

Although Norway is as far north as Alaska, it enjoys a more agreeable climate because of the modifying influence of the Gulf Stream. The fjords in the northern areas rarely freeze during the winters.

Arts and crafts are popular in Norway and flourish in spite of twentieth century interest in industrial design. Patterns are often inspired by motifs from the Viking culture, yet avant-garde designs coexist as well. Norway has an international reputation for both the old and the new and has developed an important export trade in furniture, enamelware, textiles, tableware, and jewelry that reflects both traditions in unique designs that are now associated with Scandinavian countries. These patterns characterize the national dress as well.

Norwegian folk costume has had a long and varied history but is now considered one of the most elegant of European folk dress. Because Norwegians have had long contact with Europe, many of the clothing styles of Europe were introduced to the area. Sometimes large sections of the population would accept a fashionable style from Europe, but more often only the urban centers accepted western dress and the rural people, particularly those of the distant valleys and mountains, maintained their country habits. During the latter part of the eighteenth century new styles began to develop among the people in mountain areas and fjordlands that were distinctly different from the rest of Europe. Gradually, however, western dress was accepted.

With independence in 1905 an interest and pride in things Norwegian was again manifested. Sweden was developing a keen interest in the regional dress of its area, and Norway was quick to follow this Scandinavian trend. Even people in urban centers desired some form of folk costume to wear for festivals and holidays. At first a great variety of costumes were copied and reproduced from old costumes, pictures, written descriptions, and memory. Gradually trends became noticeable and the majority of men chose a costume similar to the telemark costume of the early 1800s. The main components of the costume were a heavily embroidered long white jacket and black breeches. The women chose the hardanger costume, which consisted of a long blue wool skirt, red bodice, white blouse, and heavily decorated plastron. This outfit gradually became accepted and recognized as the "national" dress. However, extremes in decoration and detail, especially in the woman's costume, overpowered the simple dignity of the design. During the mid-twentieth century the hardanger dress gradually lost favor. Parallel with these abuses to the national dress, interest was increasing in the history and culture of each area of Norway; regional costumes began to be recognized and used more extensively. Today, Norwegian folk dress reflects the great variety of styles that were popular during the recorded history of the country. Styles have been developed for a number of regions. Often the styles represent a region no larger

67 Each region of Norway
has a distinctive dress. The
hardanger dress is noted for
its ornate plastron and hardanger work on apron and
shirt. The long skirt, so called because it falls from the
high waistline, is popular
in the Telemark and Hallingdal regions.

than a single town or parish area. All available information from past costumes, motifs, and designs is used as a source of inspiration. Many cities are still actively involved in developing a regional dress.

In Norway folk costumes are often worn on festive occasions. Young people choose the lighter colored outfits and older groups show a preference for blues and blacks. Many regions now have two or three colors deemed suitable for their costumes.

The main components of the Norwegian woman's costume are long skirt, white blouse, colorful bodice, and black shoes. Variations include elaborate aprons, one-piece bodice and skirt, wired or shaped hats, skirt bags, and elaborate belts. Men's costumes have short, elaborately decorated jackets and vests, knee breeches, colorful knee-length stockings, black shoes, white shirt, and colorful bow ties. Brass buttons and velvet trim as well as floral embroidery designs are common on men's costumes.

This varied history of Norwegian folk costume is reflected in the outfits worn in Canada. The ornate har-

danger costume is represented as well as simpler costumes from other regions. The costumes are worn for confirmations or weddings; more often, however, they are used by folk dancers, choirs, and the participants at special folk festivals. More women than men have brought costumes to Canada.

The hardanger costume is still widely used by Norwegians in Canada. Traditionally a long blue skirt was worn with a red bodice. Now a black skirt is more often combined with a red bodice, but green or brown bodices are occasionally seen. In the past a red bodice was trimmed with green and brown bands along all the edges, but now the edges are often trimmed with a metallic and/or embroidered braid. The bodice is closed at center front just above the waist and is cut so that a large horseshoe-shaped opening is left exposed. This opening is covered with a beautiful beaded plastron. Occasionally larger silver bangles and some embroidery work are seen in the geometric designs used on the plastron. The design used on the plastron is usually closely followed in the design of the belt, which

68 Costumes from eastern
Norway, in the Akershun
and Valdres regions, show
the elaborate embroidery
that is used to decorate the
costumes. The silver jewelry
is also typical.

may be long enough to reach just around the waist or may reach around the waist and extend three quarters of the way down center front. A white blouse with long sleeves and small collar is worn with the outfit. A silver brooch is pinned at the neckline. The narrow cuffs and collar are usually decorated with the white embroidery work that the hardanger region of Norway has made famous. The intricate white on white embroidery with threads drawn from small areas of both the warp and weft of the basic linen cloth is known around the world as hardanger work. By careful removal of the threads, diagonal step-like patterns can be formed. Usual patterns include stars, roses, wheels, and spokes of drawn work and intricate designs of satin stitch and eyelet work in between the holes. A white apron, again bordered with hardanger work, is always worn with the outfit. The headdress or skaut worn in Canada with this outfit does not always follow the Norwegian traditional headgear. Married women would choose between two white headdresses that would each frame the face. One is stiffly pleated and frames the face in a halo fashion, the other

is an unpleated kerchief that is securely anchored on a wing shaped frame. In Canada, women often wear a small embroidered bonnet tied under the chin with ribbons. This cap would be reserved for young girls in Norway.

A costume from eastern Norway is now replacing the hardanger costume as the most popular Norwegian "national" dress. Costumes from the county of Akershus and the Valdres region are simpler in line but more elaborately decorated with floral designed embroidery. The embroidery closely resembles the rosemaling that has been popular in southern Norway since 1700. Different areas have slight design distinctions but most favor a multicolored floral pattern. This costume from this region includes a long skirt and matching bodice, each elaborately decorated with wool embroidery. Blue and black are favorite colors, but young girls occasionally choose another color. The bodice has a smoothly curved round neckline that extends to just above the bust area. The bodice is usually fastened with lacing or silver or brass clasps just above the waistline. A silver pin known as a silja is used to fasten the top center front opening of

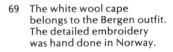

69　The white wool cape belongs to the Bergen outfit. The detailed embroidery was hand done in Norway.

the bodice. A white blouse with a high neck is also fastened with a silja or two. Blouses have long sleeves and may have either lace or embroidery trim. An elaborately embroidered skirt bag or "loose pocket" is worn hung around the waist from a belt. These skirt bags have intricate curved metal clasps of brass or silver. Black low heeled shoes always complete the outfit. Hats are rarely worn in Canada. The head covering sometimes seen here is a small cap of gold brocade.

Another uniquely Norwegian dress is the costume that originated in the mid-southern region of Telemark and Hallingdal. This costume, known as the "long skirt" or "empire skirt," closely resembles the empire line popularized throughout western Europe after the French revolution. Historically, the outfit used in Norway predated the revolution by a few years and therefore cannot be traced to this origin.

The hallingdal costume illustrates the long skirt. Today, fashionable skirt lengths determine to some extent the actual length of the skirt, but the high empire line is maintained. The tunic-like outfit with detailed rosesaum on bodice and hem border is worn without a belt for formal occasions; for less stately affairs a black leather belt may be used. Dark blue is a favorite color for the tunic. A white blouse is always worn and is closed at the neck edge with a brooch. This outfit may also include an apron decorated with rosesaum border or all over flower print and a dark jacket.

The Bergen region of Norway has developed a new outfit for women which was accepted in the late 1950s as their regional dress. The man's version of the costume is still being developed. Young girls have shown a preference for white for this outfit while dark blue and navy are chosen more often by older women. The outfit consists of the usual pieces: long full skirt, bodice, shawl, white blouse, skirt bag, and cap. The wool embroidery, although it closely follows the classical Norwegian style lines, creates the impression of a delicate, light design. Nevertheless it is crewelwork and it resembles the designs used for rosemaling. Lined fringed shawls are used with this costume in many regions. The silja may be more or less ornate, but is always worn at neck edge. The small cap is interlined to help retain the formed shape. French cuffs are used at the wrist of the blouse. Silver clasps close both skirt bag and bodice. The outfit illustrated in photographs 69 and 70 was hand embroidered and custom fit in Norway.

Most Norwegian outfits are very expensive to buy, even in Norway, because of the extensive and elaborate handwork. Many Norwegian Canadians buy a few basic pieces of the outfit on a trip to the homeland and then add additional pieces over the years. Because of this practice costumes worn in Canada may not be fully accessorized. Even so, the image of Norwegian Canadian dress is one of quiet elegance. The addition of more complete outfits can only enrich the scene.

Sweden

Swedish folk costume worn in Canada can be identified with costumes that have been accepted in hometowns in Sweden. More women's costumes are worn here than men's costumes, but there is some indication that an increasing interest in Swedish folk costume history will revive men's costumes as well. Folk costume is worn by Swedish Canadian dance groups and choirs for celebrations and for folk festivals which are constantly increasing in number. Most of the folk costumes worn in Canada have been made in Sweden and brought here by Swedish Canadians interested in preserving their heritage. These costumes authentically portray the owner's homeland region. Consequently the costumes worn in Canada are indicative of the wide spectrum of costumes worn in Sweden. Obviously it is impossible to show the great variety of folk dress worn by Swedish Canadians, but outfits discussed here are representative of Swedish folk costumes.

Swedish people have emigrated to Canada in increasing numbers during the twentieth century. Major settlements have been established in many parts of western Canada including the urban areas of Vancouver, Edmonton, Calgary, and Winnipeg. There is also a small group located around Toronto. The major North American Scandinavian settlements, however, are south of the Canadian border in the mid-northern United States.

The history of folk costume in Sweden is similar to other countries in Scandinavia and eastern Europe. Rather than a single costume that is recognized as a national dress, each community has a local dress that distinguishes that community from any other. In the past, communities were defined in terms of church parishes. All the area that was serviced by the parish wore similar dress. Traditionally, different costumes were for different Sundays and holidays of the year. Costume colors and decoration varied depending upon how festive the occasion. The practice of wearing a different costume for every holiday on the church calendar is no longer followed in Sweden, but the multitude of costumes that were worn complicates the historical research and makes it more difficult to decide upon a single costume to represent an area. A further hindrance to research arises from the fact that in urban areas where folk costume was replaced by regular western dress during the seventeenth and eighteenth centuries new folk costumes are now being developed to represent each area.

In Sweden today communities whose people had not worn folk costume for centuries are researching past costume styles for the area and attempting to develop a historically correct folk dress to represent their community. Historical accuracy is possible where complete costumes are maintained in museums or detailed descriptions are recorded. Most often, however, the reproduced costume reflects some modern interpretation of the historic dress. Sometimes pieces are accepted from a number of neighboring costumes and sometimes new fashionable lengths or styles are incorporated into the dress. Swedish craft centers have been actively involved in establishing the new costumes. The centers have revived needlecraft techniques, particularly embroidery, which is used extensively in Swedish folk costumes.

At the present time, the identifiable folk costumes in Sweden number over four hundred. Some of these are carefully preserved historic designs that were never lost in the regions, other costumes are reconstructed from accurate historic sources, and others represent a recently developed costume.

Costumes from each community differ in terms of color, fabric, decoration, jewelry, and other details. Nevertheless, the basic costume pieces throughout Sweden are remarkably similar. For example, the woman's costume almost without exception consists of wrist-length full-sleeved white blouse, sleeveless waist-length vest, neck scarf, nearly ankle length skirt, apron, and some form of head covering. Some costumes also include a waist length, long-sleeved jacket. Stockings and low heeled black shoes with some form of vamp decoration usually complete the outfit. Men's costumes are more varied in appearance because the jackets are of different lengths, but the basic outfits are usually similar. Shirts are worn with vests, jackets, or overcoat. Trousers are usually knee length and are often tied with a ribbon just below the knee. Knee length socks and black shoes are worn. The hats show a great deal of variation.

71 The Laske region has only recently reintroduced a man's and woman's costume for the The original costume was lost people accepted western dres

Everything from a black top hat to a toque-like variety is accepted as part of the folk dress. In the northern areas of Sweden the costume accepted has included some features of the Lapp dress. Especially noticeable are the leather boots with turned-up toes and the extensive use of wool fabrics.

Dalarna province in the mid-western region of Sweden has some of the oldest and best preserved costumes in Sweden. Around Lake Siljan some of the old costumes were still being worn to the parish churches in the twentieth century. Three examples from this area are shown in photographs 72 and 73-5: Råttvik, Leksand, and Floda.

The Råttvik woman's costume consists of a long blue skirt which has a front insert or breddon of horizontally striped material that has the appearance of an apron over a blue skirt. In the nineteenth century a loose apron would have been worn over the skirt; now only the skirt is worn. A short, sleeveless red bodice with rings along center front for a laced closing was traditionally worn. Today, a red and green print is often used instead. The bodice is made with wide shoulder straps that are at-

72 The rãttvik costume with its blue skirt is similar to the leksand costume with its black skirt and colored apron. Both are from the Lake District in Sweden.

tached at the back and fasten at the front with small red bows. The round-necked blouse has long loosely fitted sleeves that are gathered to a narrow embroidered cuff. A printed neck scarf is always worn and fastened with a silver pin at center front. Red stockings and small black slippers cover feet and legs. Traditionally, the red stockings were loose fitting and were worn bagged around ankles while the shoes had large tongues that extended over the front of the shoe almost to the toe. The skirt bag, worn tied around the waist, is appliqued with colors to match bodice, scarf, and blouse. Married women wear a white cap that covers the carefully tied up hair styles. The traditional rãttvik costume would be completed with a simple green jacket with red piping along the edges; however, this is rarely worn in Canada.

The man's rãttvik costume consists of yellow knee-length breeches, very dark blue vest, and long knee-length jacket with narrow red trim along the front edge. A small band of white shirt shows above the collarless vest and jacket neckline. Black stockings are worn to the knee with black cord trimmed with pompoms of wool. The outfit is completed with a low-crowned wide-brimmed hat that is decorated with a braid band and wool pompoms. Married men wear red pompoms; single men wear black pompoms.

The leksand costume at first glance appears similar to the rãttvik costume. The woman's outfit has a long black skirt which is covered at center front with a loose apron of vertical red, white, and black stripes. The traditional red bodice was decorated with vertical stripes and lacing rings at center front. In Canada, however, the bodice has embroidered decoration at side fronts. Also the traditional white neck scarf is now often replaced with a more colorful printed scarf. Traditionally, married women wore a small white cap decorated with a narrow band of black embroidery. They also wore white stockings and black slippers, often trimmed with two red pompoms. An appliqued and embroidered skirt bag was tied around the waist with a woven belt. The fine cotton blouse had full sleeves and narrow wrist bands. The outfit was often completed with a green or black jacket.

The child's dress is similar to the adult version except that the blouse and skirt are replaced with a much shorter yellow dress.

The man's leksand costume is similar in style to the råttvik costume, but it incorporates more lavish decoration. The yellow knee breeches are made from a soft chamois leather and are worn low on the hips. The black jacket and vest are decorated with rich embroidery along the shoulder line and at center front. A black hat, white stockings, black shoes, and black knee bands with red pompoms complete the outfit.

The costume from the Floda region of Dalarna had its origins in the country dress of the seventeenth century, but it also incorporates elaborate wool embroidery which was added to the costume in the 1870s. The woman's costume consists of a long black skirt with an embroidered hem border of an elaborate floral design. Red is a predominant color which is also used for a narrow band at the lower edge. A loose long apron covers the front portion of the skirt. The bodice is a multi-colored striped fabric with silver lacing rings at center front. A blue, floral decorated scarf, covering the customary white blouse, is held at center front with a silver pin. Red stockings are worn with black shoes decorated with large silver buckles. Floda women wear elaborately embroidered red bonnets and red broadcloth jackets. Each is nearly covered with multi-colored floral designs. A small embroidered black skirt bag tied around the waist completes the outfit.

For Sunday attire, men from Floda wear the usual yellow breeches, black jacket and vest, black hat and shoes. They choose blue knee high stockings and red knee bands. Their vests are double breasted and are fastened with brass buttons. For more casual wear the man's costume includes black shoes and stockings, yellow knee breeches, black vest with buttons, and green waist length jacket with red knit sleeves. Instead of the usual formal black hat, a red toque-like knitted cap is worn. Richly embroidered suspenders are worn with this outfit.

Other provinces in Sweden were not as fortunate as Dalarna in retaining their historic folk costumes. Västergötlande is an example of a province that lost nearly all ties with its earlier dress. Recently, however, a serious attempt has been made to search for and implement some folk costume traditions in the area. Västergötlande residents, because of their contacts with western Europe and their earlier acceptance of industrializa-

73 The woman from the
    Floda region of Dalarna
    wears the floda costume
    showing off the beautifully
    worked shawl and embroid-
    ered skirt bag.

74 The floda costume is
    completed with a red jacket
    covered with an embroid-
    ered floral design. The hat
    is also embroidered and
    tied with a large red bow.

75 The back view shows the
    detailed crewelwork used
    to decorate this Swedish
    dance costume.

171

tion, adopted western dress styles at the beginning of the nineteenth century. Costumes now used in the area are nearly exclusively twentieth century creations. By the early 1940s, costumes had been reconstructed for some of the northern Seven-Districts region. In the mid-1950s another wave of interest in authentic folk costume developed and a further group of costumes were produced. Since then there have been yearly additions to the accepted costumes. The Laske district costume was initiated in 1960. Individual pieces of garments from the district were identified in museums and private collections and by 1967 the woman's version of the costume was accepted. The long skirt is of striped pale blue, red, and white cotton fabric with a deep blue hem edge band. The loose apron has vertical stripes of either red or blue on a white background. The red linen bodice with eyelet holes for lacing is worn over the collarless, full-sleeved white blouse. A checked neck scarf is worn pinned at center front. White stockings and black shoes are worn. The skirt bag is sewn from the red and blue broadcloth that has a distinctive geometric design. The red silk framed cap is worn over a lace undercap.

The Laske man's costume has been only recently designed. It consists of dark blue knee breeches with pale blue knee bands and side bows, white shirt with small stand-up collar, and regular cut sleeves. The red and white striped vest with center front opening is closed with brass buttons. Overpowering the entire outfit is a large red, white, blue, and yellow checked bow tie. White socks and black shoes complete the outfit. This outfit, illustrated in photograph 71, was especially made by the wearer's sister who resides in Sweden.

8 Western Europe

**Germany
Italy
Netherlands
Portugal
Spain**

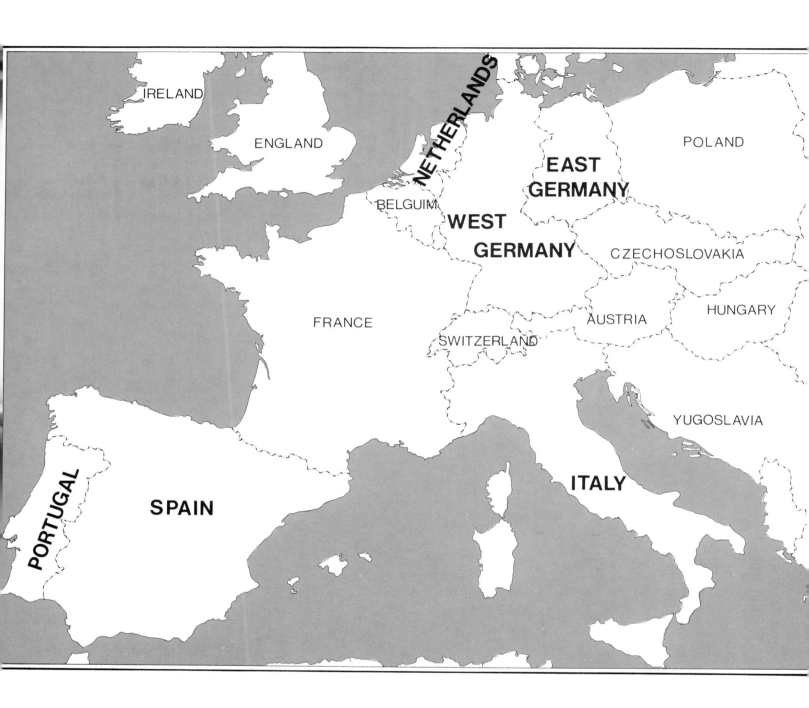

The great variety of cultures in the western area of Europe have each produced some of the most spectacular and splendid folk costumes. What is recognized most readily in Canada are the dramatic costumes of the Spanish flamenco dancers, the white huls and klompen from the Netherlands, the Bavarian short pants and hats decorated with medals from southern Germany, and the laces and satins from Portugal. Although the Canadian culture has now assimilated most of the special talents and traditions of its Western European citizens the folk costumes and individual customs observed at folk festivals remind us of the debt we owe.

The peoples from Western Europe have always been welcome immigrants to Canada. They have come here from densely populated countries that have actively encouraged emigration in many periods of their history. These lands have also been actively involved in two world wars and this fact has increased migration. Most immigrants from Italy came to Canada after World War II. They settled in Ontario. The Dutch, too, have favored southern Ontario since 1945; however, earlier Dutch settlers chose the prairies for their homes. Germans have settled throughout Canada and can be found in nearly every area from coast to coast. Again, immigrants from western Europe who came at the turn of the century settled on the prairies; those who came later favored urban centers. It has been only during the last two decades that substantial numbers of people have come from the southwest area of Europe. Prior to that, immigrants from Spain and Portugal showed a decided preference for southern and Latin American countries. Now, the urban centers of Toronto and Montreal attract the largest percentage of these new Canadians.

Germany

76 Bavarian costumes from southern Germany are worn by German dancing groups in Canada. The men's short pants, hats covered with medals, and chains of coins are typical.

Germans have contributed in many ways to the Canadian heritage. The tradition of Christmas trees and the Easter bunny were started by the Germans. Many of our favorite hymns and folk songs are of Germanic origin. Hamburgers, frankfurters, sauerkraut, and delicatessen products are German food traditions. And how can we forget the exciting fairy tales of the brothers Grimm. At folk festivals such as Octoberfest, Caravan, and Folklorama, German Canadians are further recognized by their characteristic folk costumes and their lively ethnic dances.

Nearly one and a third million Canadians claim Germanic origin. The earliest German settlement in Canada dates from approximately 1750 when a small colony was founded in Nova Scotia. Many persons of German descent moved to Canada from Pennsylvania, New York, and Georgia after the American revolution. These immigrants included many religious sects such as Mennonites who were looking for religious freedom as well as land for farming. German immigration into Canada continued throughout much of the nineteenth century.

Prior to the completion of the Canadian Pacific Railroad the major German settlements were in Ontario; after 1880, however, German immigration to the prairies greatly increased and many German immigrants came there indirectly from Poland, Austria, and Czechoslovakia. After 1950 new German immigrants favored urban centers in the industrialized areas and Toronto, Vancouver, and Edmonton now have the largest numbers of German Canadians.

Great differences in temperament are found in the people from the various regions of Germany. The sharpest contrast is between the Swabians, noted for their resourcefulness and hard-working approach to life and the Bavarians from Upper Bavaria who are noted for their rough humor and pursuit of pleasure. The Swabians have produced some of the world's great poets and intellectuals, but the Bavarians have produced great artists.

This interesting dichotomy of German characteristics has also produced distinctly different regional ethnic dress. Costumes in the northern regions are in-

fluenced by the ethnic dress of the Netherlands and the Scandinavian countries. Dark, sombre colors predominate. In south Germany, the Bavarian costume is more brightly colored. Men's costumes in most areas of Germany have the same basic components: white shirt and small bow tie, knee breeches, and long white socks or high boots. Longer trousers are not as common. A heavy topcoat or jacket is worn in northern regions. Differences in the Bavarian men's costume are obvious. They are always more ornate. Short leather breeches, known as lederhose, have shoulder braces with a center front breast strap covered with detailed embroidery. Coins often replace buttons or many coins may be hung from chains. Watch fobs and seals add more splendor. Even the small-brimmed, high-crowned felt hat in this region is adorned with flowers and feathers.

The basic costume for women that is common to most regions in Germany has a full skirt, short spencer jacket worn over a puffed sleeve blouse, white apron, and colorful kerchief. A young girl would wear a gaily decorated headpiece with many ribbons that would float around her body when she danced. A great variety of women's hats are also part of German ethnic dress. Young women from the Gutachtal region wear a straw bonnet covered with red wool pompoms which are replaced by black pompoms for more elderly ladies. The more socially important the wearer, the more pompoms she was allowed to wear. In one region of the Black Forest only married women wore hats which were known as Jochhauben or yoke hoods. This symbolized their willingness to do field work as well as housework for their husbands. Another hat from the Villingen region of the Black Forest was a wreath made from metal wire and threaded with gold and silver strands for young girls to wear. Older women wore the same wreath, but it was covered with black threads. In the Bavarian region women wore felt hats with low crowns and medium width brims decorated with an eagle feather.

Today in most parts of Germany, folk costumes have been preserved mainly in museums. However, in the Bavarian and Black Forest regions traditional folk costumes are still worn for festivals and special occasions.

In Canada, the German folk costume that is seen is nearly always Bavarian dress. German Canadian outfits are often made in Canada, but the costume is fairly accurately copied. Cost is becoming an important consideration. Men's costumes are especially expensive because they include real leather breeches. A wider variety of outfits is possible for women. A simple dirndl skirt with a blouse or the elaborate festive tracht outfit may be used. In Canada, a modified version of the tracht outfit is usually made for festivals. Green is one of the popular colors. Traditionally, homespun would be used, but this is now replaced by commercial fabrics. For example, velvet could be used for the bodice which could be laced across the front with gold or silver lacing.

In southern Germany the lacings on vests or spencers generally cover the front of the bodice from side front to side front. The bodice has a wide square neckline and the lacing rings are usually in line with the outside edge of the neckline. In this way the gold or silver lacings show beautifully across the front of the dark colored vest. Today, full circle skirts are at a fashionable length, but traditionally they would reach the ankle. A shawl is worn draped over the shoulders and tucked into the large neckline of the vest and sometimes into the shirt as well. Flowers may also be tucked into the vest neckline. The shawl and apron are color co-ordinated.

The Bavarian man's outfit is equally interesting. Gaily embroidered colorful ties are worn with white shirts. Short, above-the-knee summer breeches are also ornately embroidered as are the braces and breast piece. Calf-length hose and black shoes are worn. The felt hats have high crowns and narrow brims and are nearly always decorated with a plume of hair from the chamois, a small deer from the mountains in that area. In the winter the lederhosen are replaced with bundhosen. These are pants which reach to below the knees and are tied over a special knee-high sock. Children's costumes follow the adult fashions.

In contrast to the bright, lively folk costumes of the Bavarians, the unadorned dress of the German Mennonites and Hutterites seems very plain. Many of these people came to Canada to follow their religious ideals. They

Italy

have settled largely in rural areas on the prairies and in Ontario where they developed individual or collective farms. There are many different groups of German Canadians in Canada who follow particular religious beliefs. Each of these groups has a different dress code. To generalize very briefly they all adhere to a belief that stresses simplicity in dress. For them, ornamentation calls attention to oneself and such conduct is not acceptable. Some groups have strict dress rules; others allow more leniency. In one instance seventeenth century dress is still retained with no change, not even to the point of allowing buttons. Other groups have allowed new items to be worn so long as they have not been specifically mentioned as being forbidden. The range of dress worn by these German Canadian religious groups is from the dark, unfashionable dress of the strictest Hutterites to the modern but not high fashion dress choice of the Mennonites. These religious groups wear their established dress choice every day. Other German Canadians wear their traditional costumes only for festive occasions.

Italian Canadians celebrate folk festivals with gusto. Through their own Festival of Art and Food and the ethnic celebrations of Caravan in Toronto and Folklorama in Winnipeg, Italian Canadians have retained their traditions and maintained many modern versions of their own ethnic dress.

Even in the past, Italians enjoyed both secular and religious celebrations. Every region of the homeland had characteristics which were portrayed in their festivities. Each celebration was local and individual. Today the character of the celebrations is more general and regional peculiarities are not so obvious. Many of the major festivals focus upon the events of the Christian calendar, and holy days at Christmas, Easter, Corpus Christi, and the Feast of the Assumption are celebrated with joyful splendor. As well, each town and village honors its patron saint with annual festivals and parades. Even secular holidays warrant grand display. Everything from parades with horses and riders wearing Medieval costume to craft and modern art fairs are held regularly. Some of the major festivals have attracted a large international following, but many smaller festivals have retained only regional significance and character.

77 The green costumes from the Calabria region show the difference between the everyday and special occasion dresses from the same region. The dress from the Potenza region (center) is a modern version of an earlier twentieth-century design.

The country of Italy is almost entirely surrounded by the Mediterranean Sea, but it is also bordered by France, Switzerland, Austria, and Yugoslavia in the north. Italy is densely populated and when one considers the small area of land that is not mountainous, it is not surprising that Italians had emigrated to other countries in large numbers. For the past one hundred years migration across the Atlantic to Argentina, Brazil, United States, Canada, and Australia have amounted to over twelve million people. The United States was the favored new land, but when American immigration policies were changed in the 1920s, Canada received more Italian immigrants. Of the seven hundred and thirty thousand Italian Canadians presently living in Canada, five hundred and sixty thousand came after World War II. Currently the Toronto-St. Catherines-Hamilton area of Ontario has the largest Italian settlement with nearly half the Italian Canadians living in that area. Montreal has proved to be a favored spot as well. Distant third and fourth areas of settlement are Vancouver and Windsor.

Italians trace their ancestry to the Etruscans who founded the Roman Empire. The influence of their proud history is reflected in their varied and elaborate costumes. In some regions of Italy peasants were allowed to become quite prosperous, and they decked their costumes with expensive lace and precious and semi-precious jewelry. Sumptuary laws were subsequently written for many regions. These defined precisely the amount of fabrics and expensive jewelry allowed for various social classes. The laws were not enforced too rigorously nor were they followed precisely; however, they did have the effect of restricting the growing splendor of the Italian folk costume.

Today, lace and jewelry are still regularly and lavishly used for folk costumes but there is usually a distinction made between everyday costumes and special event costumes. The two green outfits from the Calabria region shown in photograph 77 illustrate the difference. The peasant costume for everyday wear is not as detailed nor does it use such expensive material as the dress-up costume. The gathered skirt is of green cotton and is trimmed with a lace border. The cotton blouse with the colors of the Italian flag appliqued across the front is held about the waist with a black velvet cumberband. Black shoes and stockings would traditionally complete the outfit. The pattern for this outfit was obtained in Italy, but the garments were made in Canada with modern fabrics. The costume for special occasions from the same region makes use of more luxurious fabrics and detail. The green silk skirt is pleated and sometimes has extra gathers at center back to form a small bustle. The cotton blouse has white lace trim at neck edge and sleeve hems, green silk ribbons at armscye and sleeve hem, and a red velvet vest. The vest is tightly laced to show the female form. Matched lace is used for collar, cuffs, apron, and the mantilla which covers the hair. A petticoat may also be worn. Black shoes and stockings complete the outfit. The dress style illustrated was originally used as a wedding dress about seventy-five years ago, but over the years the style has been made in different colors for other occasions as well.

The red dress from the Potenza region in the province of Lucania shows another example of the gaiety of Italian dress styles. The red wool skirt has a black velvet band along the lower edge. The matching bolero is nearly covered with a white shawl decorated with a narrow black trim along the edge. The white cotton blouse has full pleated sleeves that are tightly cuffed at the wrist.

Black satin is used for the apron, which is also pleated below the gold trim. Although the outfit was made by an Italian seamstress in Italy in 1978, the style dates around 1920. In this modern version of the outfit gold braid has been used to trim the pocket and lower edge of the apron. Traditionally gold thread embroidery would be used. Lower heeled leather shoes and white stockings are worn to complete the outfit.

Italian ladies wear much jewelry. The choice ranges from fine gold chains to ornate pieces set with pearls or precious stones.

As a rule, Italian men's outfits are not as colorful as the women's outfits; however, men may make use of brightly colored fabric for their shirts. If the shirt is linen it usually has very full sleeves and a small collar. A kerchief is often tied around the neck. Knee breeches and vest or jacket are trimmed with silver buttons. Socks may be white or colored but are usually adorned with colorful ribbons at the top. A wide sash or belt is worn around the waist. Some belts are often decorated with silver studs and fancy buckles.

Many Italian Canadians make costumes that represent their hometown region in Italy. The outfits are colorful and contribute to Canada's ethnic folk costume panorama.

Netherlands

Dutch costume is recognized today by the wooden clogs and the wing-style white hats the women wear. Currently the costume from the Volendam area in the Netherlands is widely accepted as the Dutch national dress and this costume is most often reproduced and worn in Canada.

Dutch migration to Canada started at the beginning of the twentieth century and continued until the 1930s when the depression discouraged any immigration, especially of people interested in agricultural pursuits. These earliest Dutch immigrants settled mainly around the Winnipeg area and on the prairies. After World War II the largest percentage of immigrants were from the province of Friesland. They were interested in following their agricultural interests and many of these people settled in southern Ontario where they became dairy farmers or vegetable market gardeners.

Today, the major area of settlement of Dutch Canadians is the Toronto-Hamilton area. Vancouver has the next largest population and Edmonton, Winnipeg, and Calgary each have a substantial number of Dutch Canadian people.

A large tourist industry has grown up in the Volendam region and the elegant dress from that area is readily recognized within the country and abroad. Renewed interest in costume as part of the Dutch cultural heritage is increasingly evident. The woman's volendam dress is a living costume that has gradually evolved over the years. A pleated cotton skirt, black or striped, is usually covered with a black apron that has a top band five or six inches wide. The fabric for band and tight wrap are matching and are usually a floral design on a white background. The tight wrap or kraplap is an under bodice which is visible in the square neckline of the Sunday jacket. The jacket neckline is trimmed with braid or piping. The Sunday jacket has short sleeves although the weekday jacket has long sleeves and a high neckline. The Sunday hat has a helmet-shaped crown and large, turned-up wings on either side of the face. The hat is made of heavily starched white lace to retain its shape. A three-strand necklace of large red coral beads with a gold clasp is worn. Wooden clogs or klompen complete the outfit. Traditionally, if a person was in mourning the red coral beads would be replaced with jet beads and the floral-on-white design of the tight wrap and apron band would be replaced with a dark fabric.

78 The volendam costume is internationally known as the national costume of the Netherlands. The wooden klompen and white hul with wings are easily recognized as Dutch.

The man's volendam costume includes the bragou bras, or baggy breeches, that have a flap closing in front which is fastened with silver buckles. The shirts of red and white striped material have a narrow collar decorated with black cross-stitch embroidery. A variety of jackets are worn depending upon the occasion and time of year. In summer, a striped sleeveless waistcoat is used and is covered by a short black jacket. A black knitted jersey is preferred for winter temperatures.

The Sunday jacket has a unique closing. The right side has an egg-shaped silver button and the left has a silver chain with a hook. Fastening is done by hooking the chain around the button. Volendam men wear the wooden clogs on weekdays, but they prefer a well polished black shoe with a silver buckle for Sundays. The outfit is topped with a shaggy fisherman's cap or a peaked cap.

Shawls are another integral part of women's costumes. In the past they were extremely functional and served as protection against the winds that swept across the flatlands. Now many shawls are only vestiges of their previous forms and are often seen only as small fringes inside a jacket neckline. Others have become collars on jackets.

Black and other dark colors are popular for many outfits in some areas, but other districts use printed cotton chintz as the main fabric for the skirts. Many years ago the Netherlands traded printed cotton fabrics with the Orient and imported great quantities of the fabric as yard goods and also as finished products. Regions with close ties to the trade have often incorporated printed chintz in their regional dress. Few of the fabrics and materials used in the Netherlands were made there. Lace, for example, came from the lace-making regions of France.

The outfit from the Hoorn region of North Holland shows the use of a colorful wool print for the skirt and shirt. This outfit, representing the styles popular between 1840-50, has been accented with white cotton eyelet. White handmade lace would have been the traditional fabric. The hul worn in Hoorn has a fan-shaped neck frill that stands up and away from the body. The original huls must have taken hours to maintain. The one in photograph 79 is made of modern cotton eyelet and takes three hours to iron properly with modern equipment. A coral necklace and a small silk velvet purse with a silver clasp and bead decoration complete the outfit.

The woman's outfit from the Wachgeren region of Zeeland shows the dress of the fishermen's wives. The colors of the costume are usually very dark because rigid traditions were followed for mourning and nearly always some male member of the family had been lost at sea. If the lost person was in the immediate family complete mourning was followed for one year and six weeks, then an extended period of semi-mourning after that. If the death involved a more distant relative, mourning was shortened. An uncle, for example, was mourned for six months. The outfit in photograph 79 illustrates semi-mourning because the tight wrap is light colored and a white shawl and hul are being worn. For full mourning a grey tight wrap would be used. The bonnet is actually three separate bonnets in layers. A small white hul is worn at all times and when the person goes out, the hul is covered with a blue bonnet which forms an underlining for the large white bonnet with large neck frill. A grey and white checked apron would be worn with this costume on weekdays. Black is always used for shoes and stockings.

Dutch folk dress, like other folk dress in Europe, can be traced to the country peasant dress of the various regions. The dress of some of the more isolated areas can be traced back as far as Medieval times, but most of the current styles originated as the peasant version of fashionable dress in the seventeenth and eighteenth centuries. The dress worn in the Netherlands usually reflects religion as well as region, age, marital status, and sex. Sharp contrasts are noted between Catholic and Protestant outfits. The latter often chose darker colors and less decorative styles in keeping with their reform philosophy. The trading of the Dutch East India Company and other well organized Dutch trading ventures had made some regions of the Netherlands exceptionally well off. This is reflected even in the peasant dress which uses extensive gold and silver casques, pins, and other decoration. Today, these costumes are extremely expensive and hard to obtain.

Until well into the twentieth century, Dutch people in many areas chose to wear regional dress. Gradually the men stopped wearing the costume. Children, too, were allowed to wear modern dress. Finally, the women began to switch to fashionable dress although some

79 The dark colors of
    mourning are typical of the
    costumes of the fishing
    areas where many of the men
    are lost at sea. The more
    colorful costume is from the
    Hoorn region in northern
    Netherlands.

elderly ladies still cling to the folk costume for some occasions. In the Netherlands today almost everyone has accepted modern dress for everyday wear. In some districts, however, women have retained their traditional headgear.

In Canada, the folk costume chosen nearly always represents the Volendam region. Besides being recognized internationally, it is relatively inexpensive to make in comparison with the costumes from other regions. Most Dutch Canadians have come from Friesland province but the traditional Friesland costume is almost impossible to obtain. Even the hat is now not available. The handmade lace used for the overcap cannot be had, and the traditional gold casque which covered most of the back of the head is too expensive to procure. This multilayered hat also included a couple of other layers of undercaps and some richly ornamented gold plates or needles. These plates were often decorated with precious stones, usually diamonds. A necklace of garnet or cornelian with a large center front gold locket was used to complete the Friesian outfit. Needless to

say, such finery would be beyond the means of most people today. Dutch costumes are worn here at folk festivals and to the Dutch celebration of Queen Juliana's birthday on the Saturday preceding April 30. They are also worn for special conventions and on December 5 when St. Nikolas and Black Peter make an appearance to the annual Dutch carnival occurring in February.

Every major center in Canada with a large Dutch Canadian population has a Dutch Canadian Society which is active in organizing Dutch functions. Dance and choir groups help young people to be acquainted with their cultural heritage and they promote active interest in the costumes as well.

189

Portugal

Each region in Portugal has its own distinctive dress. Even today, some costumes are still functional. In the Alentejo region, for example, cattlemen wear the red and green stocking cap, short jacket with a fox fur collar which they call samarra, and chaps. Most costumes, however, are the colorful outfits chosen for dance and choir groups. In Canada, although Portuguese Canadians obviously come from many regions of their homeland, the choirs and dance groups usually choose a costume from a single region for their entire troup. This is the case with the Portuguese Folk Dance Group of Winnipeg. They wear the Portuguese costume from Nazaré Village region when they perform for Folklorama and other ethnic festivals.

There are many people of Portuguese descent living in Canada. A dramatic increase in immigration occurred within the last twenty years and now major settlements have been established in the Toronto and Montreal areas. Today, more than sixty percent of Portuguese Canadians live in the province of Ontario. Before 1960, however, most emigrants went to Brazil which had been established at one time as the major Portuguese colony in the New World.

Portugal has experienced a high rate of emigration, mostly because of the poor wages and low standard of living which exists in many parts of the country. In fact, throughout much of the last century political instability and poor economic conditions have been the major problems.

The country of Portugal is one of the oldest established lands in Europe and is bordered by Spain to the east and north and the Atlantic Ocean to the west and south. Its culture has been greatly influenced by the Romans and the Moors when those empires were strong. Since much of its land borders on the ocean, Portugal has produced generations of sailors and was actively involved with exploring the new world, especially South America, Africa, and Asia where colonies were established. Throughout most of the last thousand years Portugal has maintained its independence; however, the country has experienced a great deal of internal strife.

In some of the northern regions of Portugal folk traditions still survive and villagers enjoy traditional songs and dances during religious festivals. Folk costume has been replaced by modern dress in most towns although some regions still wear traditional costumes for

The choir, too, wears the costume from Nazaré, but they wear the everyday dress rather than the special occasion dress worn by the dancers.

weddings and festivals. Currently the Portuguese government is attempting to promote and revive some of the folk customs to help encourage the tourist industry.

There are festivals to celebrate throughout the year. Each town enjoys a religious festival during the summer months while June tenth marks Portugal Day, and a major carnival is held in February. Dance and choir groups perform regularly at these festivals whether they are held in Portugal or Canada.

The folk costumes chosen by each dance and choir group represent many different towns in Portugal. Most costumes have a dress-up style and a plain version for everyday, but usually the Sunday-best outfit is the one represented for festivals. The costumes from the Nazaré area worn by the folk dancers feature hand-embroidered full satin skirts over full petticoats. A linear design is used on the bright red skirts, but the satin aprons are adorned with a band of floral design. The aprons, shorter than the skirts, are brightly colored. The white cotton print blouse has a yoked design that is trimmed with a red ribbon and a narrow center front bow. The head-scarves are multicolored woven kerchiefs tied in the back. White net stockings and painted shoes complete the colorful outfits. The choir also wear a folk costume from the Nazaré region. The full everyday skirt is made from cotton wool blend in a plaid pattern. Although most of the choir members choose a white blouse, a printed cotton is also worn. White knee socks and painted shoes are typically worn. Again the gaily colored satin aprons and colorful kerchiefs are worn. In Portugal a black cape would likely be worn over this costume. Many of the women watched anxiously for their fishermen to return home and needed the cape for warmth.

Men in the choir and dance groups wear a basic costume similar to that worn in many regions of Portugal. An actual representation of the Nazaré region costume would feature plaid slacks. More popular now are black slacks and vest which are worn with a white cotton or linen shirt. A bright red satin sash is tied around the waist. A black knit stocking hat is adorned with a red band around the head opening and a red pompom on the long tail. The male members of the dance group often wear the hat on a shoulder instead of on their heads if they are not actively dancing. Another type of headgear, the felt hat, is illustrated in photograph 82. This hat may be decorated with a few embroidered flowers.

81 Costumes from the Nazaré region were chosen for the Portuguese Folk Dance Group of Winnipeg. Many young people participate in this dance group which performs in various Canadian centers.

The most elaborate folk costumes of Portugal come from the Minho region. These outfits are characterized by much gold jewelry and beautiful hand embroidery. The peasant style white cotton embroidered blouse is worn with a woven vertical striped skirt of red, blue, green, and white. A black skirt is also possible. Embroidery appears on the wool apron and vest. Net stockings, painted shoes, pouch at waist, woven kerchief, and many gold chains complete the outfit. A bridal outfit from the Minho region is black and gold with a white kerchief.

The outfit from Madeira Island is worn by the young lady in photograph 82. Madeira Island is famous for its linen and embroidery work. The long sleeved white blouse may be made from either cotton or linen. The striped wool skirt is worn with a red embroidered vest which is laced at center front. A red cape is worn over one shoulder rather than wrapped around the body. The style is reminiscent of fashionable gentlemen in the seventeenth century. Knee socks or white net stockings are worn with the gaily painted shoes.

In Canada, Portuguese dancers and singers in their colorful outfits perform at folk festivals across the country.

82 The woman's costume from Madeira Island illustrates the famous linen and woven wool fabrics. The man's outfit shown here is worn by nearly all Portuguese Canadian cultural and dance groups.

Spain

Canadians think of Spain as the place of bull fights, roaring crowds, and pretty girls throwing flowers to their favorite matador. When they think of costumes it is the brilliant outfits of the torero or the frills and colors of the flamenco dancers. This popular picture of Spain is enhanced by the performing dance groups seen at Canadian ethnic festivals.

The country of Spain is situated in the southwestern part of Europe and occupies most of the Iberian peninsula. Portugal is along the western border and France is the major neighbor to the northeast. There is a small principality of Andorra between Spain and France. Spain also controls the Balearic Islands, Canary Islands, Spanish Sahara, and the cities of Ceuta and Melilla in northern Morocco.

Spain enjoyed great wealth and prestige up to the nineteenth century and this is reflected in their ethnic costume. They adopted the beautiful handmade lace and rich fabrics that were popular throughout western Europe and combined this with the luxurious fabrics of the Arab world that were their legacy from the Moors. With their new-found riches Spanish people were able to afford most of these fabrics in sufficient quantities to make exquisite folk costumes. The Arab-Oriental influence has given their dress a character quite unlike other European countries.

83 The black, red, and white outfit is the dramatic calane dress from the Sierre Morena region of Spain. The province of Granada is the origin of the beautiful lace mantilla costume.

From the Sierra Morena region comes the dramatic calane dress. The black sleeveless vest and skirt of unpressed pleats are made of wool. The long full-sleeved white blouse with small stand-up collar is traditionally trimmed with frills at center front and cuffs. A bright red cotton sash is worn around the waist. An unusual hat comes from this area. A red scarf is tied around the head with the knot at one side. Over the scarf a round black hat with a very small crown is worn. It is held on with an elastic under the chin. A red carnation is added on the opposite side of the head from the red scarf knot. Tall black boots or short boots with gaiters are worn with this outfit. The typical Spanish features of dark hair and fair skin are a striking contrast with this red, white, and black outfit.

A very different woman's costume comes from the province of Granada. The skirt of small flowered print is edged with a short skirt ruffle and a red band. The close-fitting long-sleeved black blouse is topped with a small lace shawl knotted at center front. A red velvet apron is trimmed with three horizontal rows of black lace. A white mantilla of beautiful lace is worn over an upright head comb known as a peineta. An exquisite fan of black lace with ivory and gold trim is held. White stockings and black shoes complete the outfit. The mantilla and lace shawl in photograph 83 are treasured pieces brought from Spain.

Popular in the south of Spain in the province of Seville are the folk dances known as flamenco. The dresses associated with these dramatic dances are usually floor length and have a long closely fitted bodice attached to a multi-tiered skirt. Usually, fringed shawls are worn around the neck and a flower is worn in the hair. Although often sleeveless, small puffed sleeves capped with frills are also popular. The flamenco costume from northern Spain in the province of Galicia is somewhat different. It is usually two pieces with the long skirt sometimes adorned with a hem ruffle. The blouse with elbow length sleeves is tied at center front in a large knot. With the red and white costume illustrated, red and white jewelry and flowers are worn.

The men's suits for the flamenco from the Galicia area consist of black slacks, black vest, red sash, frilled white shirt, small black boots, and sombrero cordobes, a flat-brimmed round-crown hat that ties under the chin.

In the province of Huelya, the rosiero costume is worn at the celebration that honors the Virgin Rosiero. It, too, is a long dress, usually of a polka dot or flowered print, but it is usually not flounced. Black shoes, colorful shawl, and the traditional flower in the hair are the usual accessories.

The Gypsy costume from the Sacromonte, Granada consists of tight black pants, short boots, and spotted

196

86 Children's dance cos-
tumes, too, use the dramatic
colors of the adult dress.

shirt of a soft silky fabric that is tied in a knot at center front. Although many Gypsies have been integrated into Spanish culture, many still live a nomadic life, most often in the south of Spain. Some still prefer caves for their homes.

In Canada, the lively colors of the adult costume are also portrayed in the children's dancing outfits. The young boy in photograph 86 wears the usual white shirt, red sash, and black trousers.

Spanish people have mainly chosen Latin American countries where Spanish was spoken to make their homes outside Spain. Those who have come to Canada have settled in areas around Montreal and Toronto, although there are some Spanish Canadians in other cities as well. Many festivals related to the church calendar and patron saints of each area are celebrated in Spain. Some of the most famous are the Rosiero festival, Fallas of Valencia, the April Fair of Seville, Feria, a type of fair that follows Holy Week, and the festivals honoring San Fermin in Pamplona. In Canada, Columbus Day is regularly celebrated. Folk dress is worn to these events and to other ethnic festivals as well. Today, the flounced costumes of flamenco dancers are often preferred to the more stately, elegant dress of years ago. The exquisite lace and rich embroideries of the earlier peasant costumes are now replaced with bright colored polka dots and fringed shawls.

9 Caribbean Middle East South America

Caribbean
Chile
Israel
Lebanon

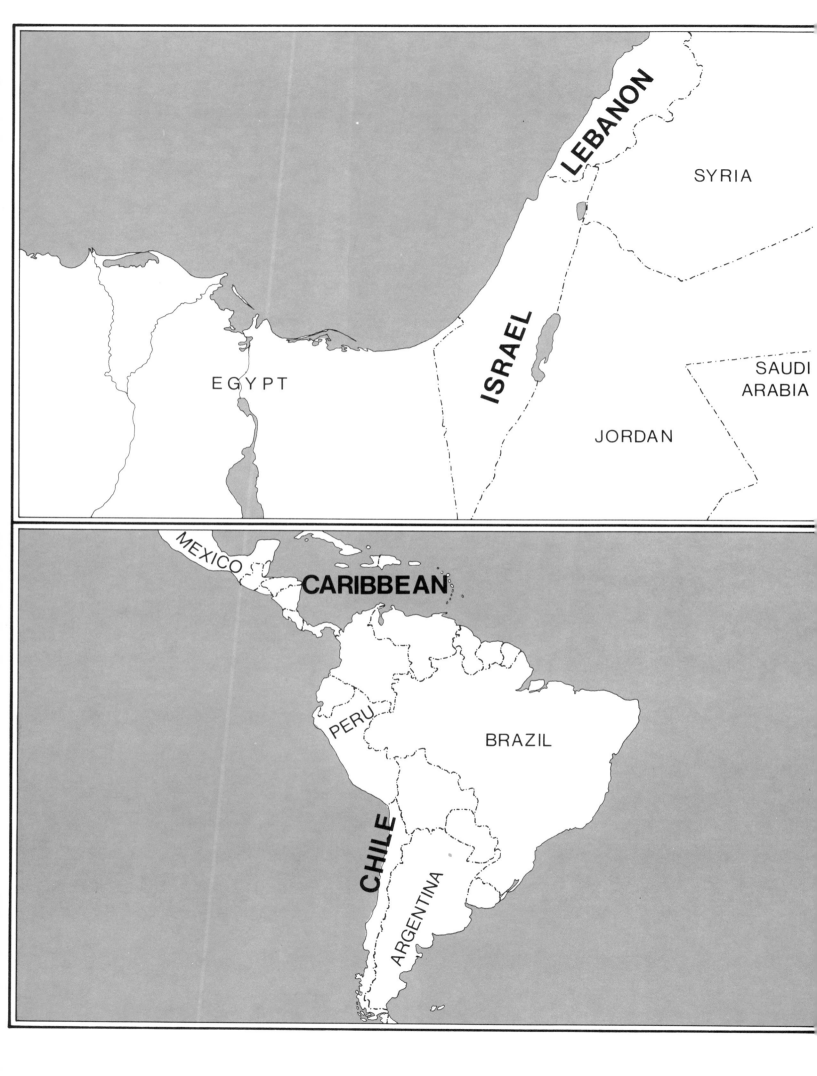

Besides the cultures already introduced, other countries have made substantial contributions to the Canadian cultural scene. How can we ignore the beautiful dance costumes and exquisite dress of the Israelis, or the colorful costumes and interesting folk customs from the Caribbean? The historic princess costume of the Lebanese and their current fashions are always deserving of appreciation. Also, in very recent times, Canadians have been introduced to the folk costumes of South America, as Chileans have come here to live. Because these countries are outside the boundaries of the other country groups they are now discussed in a group under the above heading.

There is no statistical data on the Israelis in Canada, but records do indicate that most Jewish Canadians live in the major cities in Quebec and Ontario. Less than three percent live in the Atlantic provinces, and slightly larger numbers live on the prairies and in British Columbia.

Lebanese Canadians have also chosen major urban centers. Most favored are Montreal, Toronto, and Calgary. The people from Chile are recent additions to the Canadian scene. They have chosen to live in the urban centers of Winnipeg, Regina, and Edmonton. Since the Caribbean is a culture and not a country, no statistical data on immigration is available. Substantial representation of the Caribbean Canadian population, however, is found in the Toronto-Hamilton area, Montreal, Winnipeg, and the Ottawa-Hull region.

Caribbean

The Caribbean is not a separate country but a culture that exists in the numerous islands, stretching from near Florida in the United States to the Venezuelan coast of South America. Besides the major islands of Cuba, Haiti, Trinidad, Tobago, Jamaica, Puerto Rico, Bahamas, Bermuda, and the Lesser Antilles, the Caribbean culture also incudes Guyana, Surinam, and French Guiana in South America and Belise in Central America.

The Caribbean society is an interesting blend of cultures from all corners of the world. The native population has been almost entirely replaced by immigrants from other countries. During the colonization period, slaves were brought from many of the African countries and indentured laborers were brought from Asia. With the exception of the small white minority, the ancestors of the current Caribbeans found themselves, against their own will, living in a foreign country far from their homes, families, and local customs. By necessity, these people retained what they could of their heritage and mixed it with the traditions of their new neighbors to form a distinct culture that eventually became known as Creole. The Creole culture is different on each of the many islands of the Caribbean since each island had a different geographical composition, foreign colonizer, and mix of people living there. Spanish, French, and English are the languages spoken, but many of the islands have local dialects as well. Christians, Hindus, and Muslims mix freely in Creole society. They practise their own customs and often some of the traditions from localized cults as well.

This unique blending of cultures and social systems has produced a spectacular variety of local folk traditions. For instance, the Caribbean is world renowned for its lively dances, parties, festivals, and carnivals. Most famous are the steel bands which use steel drums as instruments. The discarded drums are turned over and the bottoms are carefully pounded to form at least three, but often as many as twenty convex areas, each producing a different frequency. Played individually or in groups the steel drums are a unique Caribbean contribution to the world of music. The music, too, is distinctly Caribbean. Few people can ignor the infectious rhythm and sound. In Canada, Caribbean Canadians celebrate their festivals and the Canadian folk festivals. They have one of the liveliest and happiest folk pavilions in Winnipeg's Folklorama.

87 The man's costume
shows the comfortable form
of western dress accepted by
men in warm regions. The
traditional sari is at home
in many of the islands in the
Caribbean.

The folk costume of the Caribbean reflects the great variety of cultures that have come together there. The clothes illustrated have originated in each of the major continents of the world: Europe, Africa, and Asia. The white shirt and slacks were worn by European men as sports dress. The hot climate and the comfort of the outfit later established it as work dress to replace the suit and tie. The shirt is called either a bush jacket or shirt jack. Another man's outfit shows the West African influence. The caftan or bashiki is usually made of cotton: the photograph example is a colorful batik. Regular western slacks and footwear are worn. Both of these outfits are popular throughout the various regions of the Caribbean and were generally adopted around the time of the major thrust for independence in the early sixties.

Women's costumes show a greater diversity among the various regions. The beautiful sari reflects Asian influence. The one photographed was obtained in India in the late fifties and is hand embroidered in a tear drop design with gold thread and sequins. The colors include red, blue, and gold. Since genuine gold threads are used, laundering the sari also includes polishing the gold threads. When the sari is no longer useful, the gold threads will be removed. The midriff blouse is made from a yellow silk brocade. The sari outfit is worn as a cocktail dress or for festivals. It is also worn for Indian functions or weddings anywhere East Indians live, especially in Guiana, Jamaica, and Trinidad.

The dress worn in many of the French colonies in the Caribbean, such as Dominica, is shown in photograph 88. The long white petticoat with red ribbon and lace shows at the center front opening of the colorful skirt. The skirt is circular and ties at the waist. The front corners of the hem may be tucked into the waistline. A white peasant blouse with a wide neckline is worn. A colorful kerchief is wrapped around the head. A number of multicolored beads and bracelets always complement this costume. The skirt and kerchief may have floral or plaid design, but they will always be brightly colored.

In Canada, Caribbean Canadians wear their folk costumes to all major ethnic festivals. Their major Canadian settlements are in the Toronto-Hamilton area, Montreal, Winnipeg, and the Ottawa-Hull region.

88 The cool cotton caftan or bashiki outfit is a colorful and popular man's outfit throughout the Caribbean. The woman's costume popular in many French districts is adorned with many strings of beads.

Chile

Chilean Canadians have recently made their presence known with their lively music and gay dancing during festivals. The special event that is most enthusiastically celebrated is the Day of Chile which commemorates Chilean independence. In urban centers in western Canada such as Winnipeg, Regina, and Edmonton the Chileans settled there wear their folk costumes to Canadian celebrations as well.

The country of Chile extends along the western coast of South America from Peru to Cape Horn. It is twenty-seven hundred miles long but only one hundred and ten miles wide. The entire landscape is dominated by the Andes Mountains. Extremes is climate and geological features predominate. Winds, storms, earthquakes, volcanos, deserts, and inhospitable cold wet southern regions as well as the more moderate central region make life in Chile more complex.

The people of Chile are a homogeneous group. They are direct descendants of the native population and the Spanish people who immigrated there during the colonial period. Few other people have settled in Chile. Mestizo is the name given to these people of mixed European and American Indian ancestry.

Although Chile has been independent from Spanish domination since the early nineteenth century, both Spanish and Roman Catholic traditions have had a pronounced effect on Chilean culture. Also, sharp divisions between upper class landowners and laborers has been most evident. In recent times the military have revolted and pressed for reforms in the country. During the last few years widespread inflation and political unrest have caused many Chileans to move to North America to look for improved conditions. Those who have come to Canada have brought with them their traditions and their folk costumes to expand Canada's cultural scene.

Because of the marked climatic differences, each region of Chile has a costume that is appropriate to the weather conditions. The high altitude of most of the country forces even those people who live in regions very near the equator to wear a covering of clothing. The area in the far south is high and especially cold in July and August during the winter seasons. Such conditions have long dictated clothing styles.

In photograph 89 the couple from the southern area of Chile are dressed for the climate. The man's sweater

89 The extremes of climate in Chile account for the variety of costumes worn by the two couples. Warm wool is used in the southern regions and cool cotton is used in the north.

is handknit from wool yarn. Warm slacks tucked into heavy socks will also help protect him against the environment. The woman, too, makes use of the warmth of wool. Her shawl is knit from wool but the white shirt and dark skirt are made from any fabric. In general, warm fabrics are used for winter wear, cooler cottons for summer. Dark stockings are often chosen. By contrast, the costume from northern Chile near the equator is brighter and lighter in weight. The very full gathered green cotton skirt is attached to a narrow waistband. Yellow and red ribbons decorate the lower edge of the skirt. A white cotton blouse is worn to complement the green skirt. A hat with a medium sized crown and brim is decorated with a green band. The man's costume is a cool white outfit accented with a blue neck scarf and blue and white belt. In this region cotton is the preferred fabric and shoes are not always worn.

Photograph 90 shows a variety of costumes from the north and central regions. All are worn in Canada for dancing and festivals and were made here in 1977. The men from the north region wear white cotton trousers and white shirt. Their neck scarves and belts are color co-ordinated with the outfit worn by their partner. The women wear the full skirt and matching shawl over a white blouse. Often a head scarf is worn wrapped around the head and tied at the back. A variety of footwear is acceptable.

In the central region a printed dress with a full gathered skirt, elbow-length sleeves, and a fitted bodice with a large round neckline trimmed with white cotton lace is chosen. The skirt is covered with a white apron with a frill around the edge. The man from the central region wears an outdoor outfit. His plaid shirt and tan vest are worn with dark trousers and an elaborately woven waist sash. A flat-brimmed sombrero is tied under the chin. Both men and women carry a white handkerchief when dancing.

The Chilean costumes are an interesting blend of Spanish and Indian styles. Each dress is functional and exhibits its own peculiarities which are characteristic of the area.

90 The dress from the central region shown on the right is typical of peasant outdoor dress. The other three couples show the dress worn in the northern areas near the equator.

209

Israel

92 The embroidered yellow caftan and the short blue caftan are costumes typical of Israel today. The long blue sheer caftan and the man's long caftan are outfits worn by the Moroccan Jews from Tangiers.

Following the United Nations partition of Palestine between the Jews and Arabs on May 15, 1948, Israel emerged as the first Jewish state to be established in over two thousand years. For the Jewish people this was the fulfillment of an historic religious belief in God's promised land. The new state of Israel is bordered by Lebanon, Syria, Jordan, Egypt, and the Mediterranean Sea.

Although Jewish people started to settle in the present-day area of Israel as early as 1880, and many other Jewish people followed them before 1948, the real influx of settlers was between 1948 and 1970 when the population increased from sixty-five thousand to nearly two million people. Israel must be one of the few countries where over fifty percent of its population was born elsewhere. Jews from around the world immigrated to their new country. Many of the survivors from the Nazi occupation of Europe and those that were subjected to anti-sematic feelings elsewhere chose Israel as their new home.

But Israel's population is not all Jewish. Muslims account for twelve percent of the people who live there,

91 The colors of the flag of Israel are used in the modern dance costumes worn in Canada by the Chai Folk Ensemble.

94 The brown and gold Yemenite costume would be worn by a bride to the party before the wedding. In the background, the costume of a shepherd is shown.

Christians for two percent, and Druzes and other small religious sects for about one percent. Even the eighty-five percent of the population that is Jewish does not share a common cultural background. In fact, these people do not even share a common religious background. There are two chief rabbis in Israel. One heads the Ashkenazi rite (for Jews from eastern and central Europe); the other heads the Sefardi and Oriental rite (for Jews from the Mediterranean region and from the Middle and Far East). Folk customs that are associated with the Jewish faith and traditions from many other countries have been brought to the new country. This uncommon blending of cultures from around the world has resulted in a unique culture for Israel. An interesting interpretation of folk songs and dances has resulted. Another factor to be considered is that the rural Arab population and the Oriental Jews have preserved more of their original folk cutoms than have other Israelis. When discussing Israeli traditions, therefore, a distinction must be realized between the old Jewish customs and the culture of the new country. Both are an integral part of the cur-

93 Yiddish woman's costumes are shown with the costume of a Yiddish rabbi.

212

rent traditions. The blue and white dancing costumes in photograph 91 represent modern Israel. They utilize the national colors of the Israeli flag. The woman's costume consists of a white body suit and a circular skirt. The skirt has four panels. two of each color. The man wears a white shirt and blue trousers. The costumes are made in Canada and used strictly for folk dancing.

The yellow caftan in photograph 92 was obtained in Israel. The caftan has long been accepted dress in this area of the world and can be made from either cotton or silk. Israel is known for its rich embroideries and these are well illustrated on this festive outfit. The man wearing the hip-length blue caftan also models an Israeli costume worn for less formal occasions. The caftan is cotton and features some embroidery. The costume worn by the Moroccan Jews from Tangiers is also a caftan. The sheer silk fabric of the woman's outfit is decorated with glittering beadwork and embroidery and would be worn for formal occasions. The ankle length man's caftan is made of cotton and would be worn only for informal occasions.

The colorful outfits in photograph 94 are costumes based on the traditional Yemenite costume. They consist of black tights, a shirt, a coat, and a headpiece. Traditionally, such an outfit would be worn by a bride to a pre-wedding party. The shirt has a gold metallic embroidered bib which complements the gold trim on the coat and the headpiece. The coat is made of a denim sheeting or similar stiff fabric. The headpiece consists of a chiffon veil and a cap, which would have originally been decorated with coins. Traditionally, the veil would have been used to cover the lower part of the face for part of the party. The hair was always completely concealed. Much jewelery would be worn. The man in the same photograph represents a shepherd from biblical times. He wears the white pantaloons that are draped from a single flat piece of fabric plus a bolero-style jacket. The hat is functional, to protect him from the sun.

Photograph 93 represents the Yiddish costume of the Orthodox Jew. The women dress very modestly with their long skirts, long-sleeved, high-necked blouses, and kerchiefs. The skirt can be made from a cotton or

Lebanon

a brocade, depending upon the occasion. The blouse is cotton or wool and the scarf is wool. An apron with a woven design completes the outfit. These costumes were made in Canada, but the same type of costume is worn by Yiddish people in Israel. The man represents a Yiddish rabbi. His outfit includes trousers, a coat, and a hat. Two types of coat may be worn: wool for out-of-doors or a lightweight silk for inside the synagogue. The slacks and coat were made in Canada. The hat made of velvet and trimmed with fur is an original. It was donated by a Hasidic rabbi.

Although few Israelis have chosen to migrate to Canada since the formation of the country, many Jewish people from North America have gone to Israel to live on the kibbutz. In the new country, song and dance continue to be an expression of past and present experience. Today, Jewish people living in Canada present the culture of Israel at folk festivals. It is mainly through Jewish Canadian cultural organizations and dance groups that such folk costumes are displayed in Canada.

Canadian concepts of Lebanese dress picture exotic belly dancing costumes or the flowing robes of romantic sheiks. Actually these fanciful ideas have basis in fact. Lebanese costume is both dramatic and beautiful. A great variety of Lebanese folk costumes are worn in Canada for large folk festivals such as Folklorama and Caravan. However, festivals that are specific to Lebanese holidays are more often celebrated in the United States than in Canada.

The country of Lebanon is one of the smallest sovereign states in the world. Nestled between Syria, Israel, and the Mediterranean Sea, the area has been the site of some of the oldest and most powerful civilizations in known history. Phoenician, Greek, Roman, and Byzantine cultures have all left their influences. It was not until the twentieth century that the modern state was formed. Lebanon became a republic in 1926 and achieved independence from France in 1943. It is now a member of the Arab League.

The peoples of Lebanon are a heterogeneous group. Traces of the early empires in the area can still be found there, as well as elements from the Crusades of the Middle Ages and from Arab culture. Many Arab tribes moved into the area from the Arabian desert while Armenians dominated the hilly regions. Today, the population is almost equally divided between Christians and Muslims.

As is usually the case, when two or more great cultures are shared, great artistic achievements are made. Lebanon has been particularly successful in producing some great achievers in the fields of ballet, drama, symphony, and opera. With the establishment of an independent country and recognition given to the achievements of local talent, pride of nation has made many young artists devote more of their time to the revival of national folk arts. Folk songs, dance, and poetry are receiving renewed interest and traditional crafts are being refined. The annual Baalbek International Festival staged with the ruins of Jupiter as a backdrop is now attracting worldwide attention for the quality of its music. Independence Day is celebrated in July, but many of the small regional festivals celebrated with such enthusiasm before the civil war have not as yet been revived.

Folk costume has also been considered with renewed interest. The diaphanous and flowing belly dancing costumes are familiar all over the world. Less recognized is the Bedouin dress of the nomads of the desert and the dress of the Druze, a religious sect living in the mountains of Lebanon. Both make use of long flowing robes. The Bedouins, for protection against the desert heat, cover themselves with shawls and robes of wool. Beautiful embroidered panels often adorn the main tunic. Traditionally, the tunics are an off-white color and the embroidery is dark blue or black. The head is always covered with a shawl. Ornate metal bangles are popular jewelry pieces. The Druze costume is layered for warmth in the mountains. Very full baggy pants are worn with two or three layers of shirts and a long pullover jacket. Natural fibers and natural dyes are used to obtain the beautifully woven striped designs of the tunics and jackets. Embroidery is occasionally used to decorate the parts of the under tunics that show around the center front openings.

Photograph 95 shows two outfits still worn in Leban-

95 The currently fashionable Lebanese caftan and man's outfit are shown with the traditional princess costume from the Beirut area. The gold-embroidered caftan is worn in Canada to cocktail parties and for other dress occasions.

on today. The black velvet caftan with the exquisite gold embroidery would be worn with gold slippers for evening wear. It was also admired as evening wear in Canada when it was first brought back from Lebanon about four years ago. The man's outfit also portrays a current Lebanese fashion for the wealthy sheik. The white shirt and slacks and red bow tie are of modern design. The red sash is made from silk and the fez or tarboosh has a black tassel at the back. The tarboosh, worn by Muslim men, may be worn by itself or under the turban. The ankle length robe is of fine wool and flows freely around the man. The inside front edges are often decorated with applique and embroidery that shows when the wearer moves. This basic outfit comes in many color schemes and is worn in every part of Lebanon. The outfit illustrated was obtained in Lebanon in 1978.

The Lebanese princess outfit is from the region of Beirut and shows the splendor of Lebanese costumes from the past. The Beirut area today is westernized but for folk festivals in both Lebanon and Canada the elaborate princess dress is often worn. The costume is multi-layered. A sheer white lace dress is worn over a colored slip. A long coat of pink silk brocade is worn closed at center front between the bust and waist area. The long pagoda-shaped sleeves reach to the wrist. Under the dress, lace pantaloons are held up with a belt. The most dramatic aspect of the costume is the tall peaked hat which is almost identical to the fifteenth century hennin worn by fashionable ladies of Europe. The lace veil hangs from the point and reaches to wrist length. The green band around the bottom of the hat is known as a donut. Gold or silver slippers would complete this costume. The costume illustrated was obtained in Lebanon in the early 1970s and is worn at Lebanese special events and at Folklorama.

Costume References

Anderson, Ruth Matilda. *Spanish Costume Extremadura.* New York: Hispanic Society of America, 1951.

Berg, I. A. and G. H. Berg. *Folk Costume of Sweden: A Living Tradition.* ICA bokforlacj Nåsteras.

Boucher, Francois. *20,000 Years of Fashion.* New York: Harry N. Abrams, Inc.

Clabburn, Pamela. *The Needleworker's Dictionary.* New York: William Morrow and Company, Inc., 1976.

Davenport, Millia. *The Book of Costume.* New York: Crown Publishers, Inc., 1976.

Facts About Korea. Thirteenth Revised Edition. Gwanghwamun: Korean Overseas Information Service Inc., 1977.

Fairservis, Walter A. Jr. *Costumes of the East.* Connecticut: The Chatham Press, 1971.

Fox, Lilla M. *Folk Costume of Western Europe.* London: Chatto and Windus Ltd., 1969.

Gehret, Ellen J. *Rural Pennsylvania Clothing.* York, Penn: Liberty Cap Books, 1976.

Gervers, Molnar V. *The Hungarian Szűr: An Archaic Mantle of Eurasian Origin.* Ontario: Royal Ontario Museum, 1973.

Grimble, Ian. *Scottish Clans and Tartans.* New York: Hamlyn.

Haire, F. H. and C. Moser. *The Folk Costume Book.* New York: A. S. Barnes and Co., 1926.

Korea 1977-78. Asian News Center, Seoul, Korea.

Keywan, Zonia and Martin Coles. *Greater than Kings.* Montreal: Harvest House, 1977.

Kulisic, Spiro. *Traditions and Folklore in Yugoslavia.* Beograd: Jugslaveja, 1966.

Kunio, Y. *Japanese Manners and Customs.* Tokyo: Obunsha, 1957.

Kurelek, W. and A. Arnold. *Jewish Life in Canada.* Edmonton: Hurtig Publishers, 1976.

Leeming, Joseph. *The Costume Book.* Philadelphia, N.Y.: J. B. Lippincott Co., 1938.

Mann, Kathleen. *Peasant Costume in Europe.* London: Adam and Charles Black, 1937.

Metropolitan Museum of Art. *History of Russian Costume from the Eleventh to the Twentieth Century.* New York.

Miers, John. *Travels in Chile and Lo Plata.* New York: Ams Press, 1826.

Minnich, H. B. *Japanese Costume and the Makers of Its Elegant Tradition.* Tokyo: Charles E. Tuttle Co., 1963.

Olson, Eleanor. *The Textiles and Costumes of India: A Historical Review.* Washington: The Newark Museum, 1965.

Stewart, J. S. *The Folk Arts of Norway.* Madison: The University of Wisconsin Press, 1953.

Ukrainian Canadians. Edmonton: Ukrainian Women's Association of Canada, 1976.

Valeton, Elsa M. *Dutch Costumes.* Amsterdam: De Driehock.

Vilppula, H. and T. Kaukonen. *Folk Costumes and Textiles.* The National Museum of Finland.

Wilcox, R. Turner. *Folk and Festival Costume of the World.* New York: Charles Scribner's Sons, 1965.

Yacopino, Feliccia. *Threadlines Pakistan.* Karachi Elite Publishers Ltd., 1977.

Zunic-Bas, L. *Folk Traditions in Yugoslavia,* Ten Tours.

Costume Glossary

Aboyne costume The traditional Scottish woman's dancing costume. It consists of a checked skirt, velvet vest, white blouse, and strip of fabric matching the skirt which is pinned to one shoulder.

Ahoti A loin cloth worn by Indian men.

Alampay A scarf worn over the head and shoulder as part of the female costume for the candle dance of the Philippines.

Assomption sash A fingerwoven sash worn as part of the French Canadian man's costume. It is also known as ceinture flêchée or arrowhead sash.

Baldrick A strap, often of leather, that is worn across the chest, under one arm, and over the opposite shoulder. It is often part of a military uniform.

Barong tagalog A Filipino man's shirt decorated with delicate embroidery and cutout work. This term is often used to describe the man's complete outfit.

Baro't sayo A woman's costume from the Philippines consisting of a skirt (sayo), a blouse (camisa), and (panuelo).

Bashiki A caftan worn by men in the Caribbean. The garment was influenced by West African costume.

Bragou bras Baggy breeches or trousers with excess fullness worn as part of the man's volendam costume from the Netherlands.

Brau A handwoven belt worn by men and women in Romania. It is also known as chinga.

Breddon A front panel of horizontally striped fabric inserted in a long skirt. It is part of the råttvik woman's costume from Sweden.

Brogues Scottish dancing slippers.

Broigins Leather boots worn in Ireland.

Bundhosen Leather trousers which reach to below the knees and are tied over a knee high sock. They are part of the German (Bavarian) man's winter costume.

Calane dress From Sierra Morena, Spain. Outfit has black wool vest and skirt, frilled white blouse, red sash, head scarf and hat.

Camaşe An embroidered blouse worn by Romanian women.

Camisa A loose-fitting blouse worn as part of the woman's Filipino outfit, the baro't sayo.

Capot A long-sleeved hooded overcoat which was worn by early French Canadian settlers and explorers.

Catrinţa A wool wraparound skirt worn by Romanian women. It is almost entirely covered by metallic thread embroidery.

Ceinture flêchée A fingerwoven sash worn as part of the French Canadian man's costume. It is also known as assomption sash.

Chatelaine bag A bag-like purse which usually has some form of metal clasp that may hook to a belt. It is often decorated with metallic thread, braid, or embroidery. Worn by Dutch women.

Cheongsam A tight-fitting, sheath-like dress with a mandarin collar worn by Chinese women. It is often called the Hong Kong sheath in Canada.

Chi'i-fu A floor-length collarless robe worn by the Chinese Emperor and his court. It has long sleeves and horseshoe-shaped cuffs. The fabric is elaborately decorated with ancient symbols. The ch'i-fu is also called the dragon robe.

Chima A long, full, high-waisted wraparound skirt worn by Korean women.

Chinga A handwoven belt worn in Romania by both men and women. It is also known as brau.

Chogori A short bolero blouse worn by Korean women. It is tied at center front and has long full sleeves which are cut narrow in the wrist area. It also refers to a jacket worn by Korean men.

Choli A blouse worn with the sari of India and Pakistan. It is usually small and tight, but the actual size and shape depend on the age of the wearer and the geographical location of the homeland.

Contusze costume A luxurious Polish man's costume which reflects the court dress of the sixteenth and seventeenth centuries.

Croiss Fabric belt worn like a sash around the waist. Often matched the kilt.

Dirk A combination of hunting knife and small knife and fork for eating which is carried on a belt by Scottish men.

Drugget A homespun fabric consisting of a mixture of linen and wool. Made and worn by early French Canadians. Also known as linsey-woolsey.

Dupatta A sheer fabric scarf, just over two meters long, that is either worn in a gentle V around the neck with the ends draped over the shoulders or worn draped over the head. It is worn by Pakistani and Indian women.

Fez A cap in the shape of a truncated cone worn by men and women in many of the Balkan States.

Fuho A black wraparound silk kimono worn by a Buddhist priest in Japan.

Furisoda A long-sleeved kimono worn only by unmarried women in Japan.

Gamiz A loose-fitting, knee-length, long-sleeved tunic worn by Pakistani and Indian women. It is part of the shalwar-gamiz outfit.

Gaiters Cloth or leather leg covering reaching from instep to ankle, mid-calf, or knee.

Gharara An outfit worn by Pakistani and Indian women for formal occasions and weddings. The garment is bifurcated but leaves the image of a long full skirt.

Glengarry bonnet A kind of cap high in front and sloping towards the back. Worn by men in the Scottish highlands.

Hakama Full-cut silk trousers which were traditionally worn by upper class Japanese women but are now worn chiefly by Japanese men as ceremonial dress.

Hardanger dress Recognized as one of the national Norwegian dresses for women and features hardanger embroidery work. It consists of a long blue wool skirt, red bodice, white blouse, and heavily decorated plastron.

Hardanger work Name refers to the white on white embroidery work that the Hardanger region of Norway has made famous.

Hufa A fitted short vest worn by Icelandic women. It is part of the upphlutur costume.

Hul A woman's white lace hat of the Netherlands.

Jelek A small bolero-like jacket worn in Serbia. It is ornately decorated with embroidery or intricate weaving.

Jochhauben A hat worn by German women in one region of the Black Forest. Wearing the hat symbolized a woman's willingness to do field work as well as housework for her husband.

Jusi A gossamer banana fiber that was traditionally used to make the sleeves of the national Filipino woman's dress.

Kameez A loose-fitting, knee-length, long-sleeved tunic worn by Pakistan and Indian women. It is also known as gamiz.

Kansaski A hairpiece worn by Japanese women.

Kapta A tunic worn by Lapp men and women. It has long sleeves, little or no collar, and a gathered skirt. It can also be called a peski, depending on the location.

Kimono The basis of Japanese dress for men and women. It is made entirely of rectangular pieces of fabric.

Klompen Dutch wooden clogs.

Koloshnik A headdress which is part of the South Russia woman's costume. The shapes of the headdress and the types of decoration on them vary according to the region of Russia.

Kosode A small-sleeved garment worn by married women in Japan.

Kraplap Also tight wrap, is an underbodice worn as part of the woman's volendam dress of the Netherlands.

Kurta A light loose shirt worn in Pakistan and India. It can be made of silk, linen, or cotton and is decorated with embroidery and braid.

Lederhosen Short leather breeches worn as part of the German (Bavarian) man's summer costume. They are supported by shoulder braces that are gaily embroidered.

Lungi A shawl worn by Indian men.

Maguli An Indian woman's outfit which originated in the Mogul courts of the fifteenth to nineteenth centuries. It includes choordor pyjamas, dupatta, blouse, and slippers.

Malong A tubular-shaped garment worn by women in the southern part of the Philippines.

Mantilla A lace veil worn by Italian and Spanish women.

Maria Clara An outfit that was worn by Philippine women in the late 1880s that included an exquisitely embroidered sheer camisa and panuelo and a velvet or silk sayo. Today the term "Maria Clara" is usually used to describe a less formal outfit.

Mutåkas Pointed reindeer shoes worn by men and women in traditional Lapp costume.

Obi A sash wrapped around the outer kimono of Japan. The ends are tied at center back and the long ends are tied into a knot or bow.

Obijime The narrow cord worn over the obi which is fastened at center front with an elaborate pin or in a tight knot. It is part of the Japanese kimono costume.

Pagri A turban worn by Indian men which can be wrapped in several styles around the head.

Paharen A light loose shirt worn by Indian and Pakistani men. It can be made of cotton or silk and is decorated with embroidery.

Paji Baggy, wide trousers which fit snuggly at the ankle. They are worn by Korean men.

Panuelo A shawl draped over the shoulders to form a high neckline at center back. It is worn by Filipino women as part of the baro't sayo outfit.

Pastalas Small leather slippers worn in Latvia.

Peineta An upright head comb worn under the mantilla by Spanish women.

Pekko Protection for the hands which forms part of the work outfit of a Japanese female field worker.

Peski A tunic worn by Lapp men and women. It has long sleeves, little or no collar, and a gathered skirt. It can also be called a kapta, depending on the location.

Peysuföt Term refers to the dress-up costume of the Icelandic female.

Pina A pineapple fiber that was traditionally used to make the sleeves of the national Filipino woman's dress.

Plaid Large rectangular piece of fabric with checkered pattern worn by highlanders of Scotland.

Plakhta A wraparound skirt of colorful woven fabric worn by Ukrainian women as part of the poltava-kiev outfit.

Plastron A type of dickey worn at center front of an open bodice.

Poias A wide woven belt worn by Ukrainian men as part of the poltava-kiev outfit.

Poneva A skirt characteristic of the South Russia woman's costume. It is made from three lengths of checked woolen homespun. Often it is not closed at center front so as to expose the long shirt under the apron.

Pukko A form of hunting knife carried in a belt worn by Lapp men and women.

Samarra A short jacket with a fox fur collar worn by cattlemen in the Alentejo region of Portugal.

Sarafan A joined bodice and skirt worn by women in northern Russia. It may be made of velvet, brocade, silk, or linen.

Sari A flat piece of fabric about one meter wide and between four and a half and six meters long that is wrapped around the body to form a gown.

Sartza An apron worn at the back of a skirt by Greek women on the Isle of Crete.

Sayo A floor length full skirt worn by Filipino women as part of the baro't sayo outfit.

Sgian dubh A small knife worn tucked into the right hose between the stocking and the leg. It is part of the Scottish man's costume.

Shai Small slippers worn by Indian women as part of the maguli outfit.

Shalwar A pair of trousers which are gathered at the waist by a drawstring and tapered to a snug fit at the ankle. They are worn by Pakistan and Indian men and women.

Shalwar-gamiz An outfit worn by Pakistan and Indian women. It consists of shalwar, gamiz, and dupatta.

Shan A silk jacket worn by Chinese men and women as part of the traditional costume.

Silja A silver pin used to fasten the top center front opening of the blouses worn by women in various regions in Norway.

Skaut A Norwegian woman's headdress. Traditionally it was either pleated and framed the face halo-fashion or an unpleated kerchief anchored on a wing-shaped frame. In Canada, a small embroidered bonnet is regularly worn instead.

Skautbuningur Name refers to the festive dress of the Icelandic woman. It is the most lavish and expensive costume of Iceland.

Skirt bag A loose pocket worn hung around the waist from a belt. It is part of the female dress in many regions of Scandinavia.

Skyrta A long heavy wool serge or black velvet skirt worn by Icelandic women as part of the upphlutur costume. It is embroidered around the hem with gold and silver floral designs.

Sõlg Name refers to the small ball buttons on the blouse worn by Estonian women from the island of Mustjala.

Sombrero cordobes Flat-brimmed round crown hat that ties under the chin.

Sorcerer's cap The traditional hat worn by men of Lapland. It has four large stuffed points which are worn pointed in each direction for married men or all pointed forward for single men.

Sort Consists of front and back panels worn apronlike over a skirt. It is worn by women in some regions of Romania.

Sporran A pouch worn by Scottish men with the kilt. It is attached on a chain around the waist.

Szűr A long straight-cut coat or mantle that originated in Hungary. It was worn by men as a coat but could also be used as a sleeping bag, saddle bag, or tent.

Tabi Socks worn as part of the Japanese traditional dress. They are made with big-toe stalls to allow proper fit in the thong-type sandal.

Tapis A hip scarf that is worn as part of the woman's costume for the candle dance of the Philippines.

Tarboosh A hat worn by Muslim men either by itself or under a turban.

Tartan Wool cloth in a plaid pattern consisting of varied colored bands crossing at right angles. Worn in Scottish highlands.

Terno The Filipino woman's national dress characterized by large butterfly sleeves.

Tika A bright red spot on the forehead of Indian women. It was originally a symbol of wifehood, but now unmarried girls occasionally adorn themselves in this way.

Tracht A festival dress for German girls.

Upphlutur Name refers to the everyday costume of Icelandic women's dress. It is now considered the national dress of Iceland.

Wagesa A stole-like garment worn around the neck as part of the Japanese Buddhist priest's robes.

Zori A thong-type sandal that has a small strap between the first and second toe. It is worn by Japanese men and women.

Zubun A knee-length, sleeveless, collarless jacket worn in Serbia. It is ornately decorated with embroidery or intricate weaving.

Zywiec costume A woman's costume from the region of Zywiec, Poland. It reflects the court dress of the sixteenth and seventeenth centuries.

Contributors

Caribbean
Yvonne Ballentyne
Angus Bramadat
Donovan Hale
Sita Singh
Inskip Spencer

Chile
Jimy Argel
Eva Canejo
Carniere Gáher
Esteban Gáher
Ludania Gáher
Claudio Molina
Marisol Muñoz
Patricia Muñoz
Rodrigo Muñoz
Marcelo Rosales
Leon Salenzuela
Mario Sosa
Eliana Soto

China
Keith Au
Mrs. Lucia Au
Nola Chao
Lolita Gin
Loretta Gin
Deanna Lee
Mabel Lee
Margaret Lee
Philip Lee
Sandra Tan
Jennifer Tse
Angela Yeh
Emerald Yeh
Dr. and Mrs. Martin Yeh

Croatia
Steve Jankac
Anita Kanpic
Betty Starcevic
Rev. Dominic Tomic

Denmark
Karen Jacks (Osted)
Hans and Elise Osted
Shira Wood

English
David Edwards
Elizabeth Goossen
Archie Nixon

Estonia
Hilda Sults

French Canadian
Raymond Normandeau
Valerie Normandeau

Finland
Rolf Lilje-Gren
Marlene MacDonald
Maire Rainonen
O. Suominen
Mary Syrjala

Germany
Egon Delfing
Anita Frank
Roy Hartfiel
Rudy Hartfiel
Joseph Kolbe
Elizabeth Kurtz
Will Kurtz
Fred Oberbuchner
Gerald Oberbuchner
Claudia Petsch
Monica Weber

Greece
Helen Bastounis
Anna C. Cholakis
Mrs. Helen Cholakis
John Calogeris
Joanne Grafos
Janis Mikos
Chrysan Paulos
Nancy Vardalos
John Vlahios

Hungary
Rev. Luis Aday
Eva Baricz
Julika Baricz
Klara Baricz
Tibor L. Boda
Julius Gross
Rosemary Olah
Father Paldeak
Agnes Taubner

Iceland
Lilja Arnason
Gudrun Blondal
Lilja Lecko

India
Rasheda Ahsanuddin
S. Sarkar
Sewa Singh Sidhu

Ireland
Seán Campbell
Brenda Carruthers
Lynn Thompson

Israel
Mimi Breitman
Gina Frieman
Renee Kaplan
Erna Kinnel
David Lavitt
Gary Levine
Jill Lhotka
Nenad Lhotka

Jerry Maslowsky
Sid Ritter
Abbie Schacter
Randy Silver
Sherri Walsh
Paula Weiss

Italy
Marietta Pellettieri
Maria Rondinone
Connie Scerbo

Japan
Satoko Hayashi
Yoshiharu Hayashi
Kimi Hisanaga
Keri Ito
Mrs. Ito
Heather Kaita
Denise Katai
David Nashimura
Tannis Nishibata
Kim Okano
Michele Oye

Korea
Chen Pyo Hong
Cho Ja Hong
Choon Ja Lee
Heeman S. Lee
Katherine Jeanhyo Lee

Lapland
Lisa Hicks

Latvia
Rita Blosmanis
Lilita Klavins
Zinta Radovskis
Charles Redovsky
Paul Rutulis
Paul Tyzek
Tamara Tyzek

Lebanon
Kelly Farrage
Wafan Farrage
Marjory Forzley
Janis Winter

Lithuania
Vinces Janoska
George Valaitis

Netherlands
Marianne Niesink
Joan Potter
Carol Ten Berk de Boer
Gerrit Ten Berk de Boer
Harry Van Helden

Norway
Sigrid Bretsen
Inger H. Lewis
Florence Overgaard
Jessie Sutherland
Shirley Syslak

Pakistan
Tahira K. Hira

Philippines
Butch Andojera
Tessie Briones
Marilou G. Camaclang
Pedrito F. Primolo
Roger M. Marcelo
Resty Tarul
Eileen M. Tiongco

Poland
Mrs. Langtree
Tadz Liusz
Teresa Lobczuk
Christopher Lorenz

Portugal
Celestino Alpestana
Celia Alpestana
Elizabeth Alpestana
Jack Alpestana
Luis Anica
Adelia Branco
Anna Camilo
Tina Camilo
Elizabeth Chagas
Celia Coelho
Dulce Coelho
Cesario Correia
Isabel Cruz
Nancy Cruz
Annette Elvas
Beatrice Elvas
David Elvas
Bill Fernandes
Susie Fernandes
Gina Ferreira
Elizabeth Garanhel
Sergio Goncalves
Joe Guerra
Manuel Guerra
Carlos Jorge
Luis Jorge
Paulo Jorge
Fatima Lopes
John Lopes
Manuela Martins
Sandy Martins
Fatima Melo
Jose Neto
Lidia Neto
Odede Neto
Annabelle Neves
Manuel Rocha
Abilio Rodrigues
Joe Rodrigues
Arlette Santos
Tony Santos
Isabel Sebastiao
A. Tavares
Bradley Tavares

Helen Tavares
Leonor Tavares
Jerry Vieira
Manuela Vieira

Romania
Mary Franucishen
Alexandra Holunga
B. M. Holunga
N. W. Holunga
Carl Pentlichuk
Ana Russell

Russia
Irma Christ
Vera Weremiuk

Scotland
Maureen Burnham
Catherine Carlson
Michael Lynch
Robin Lynch
John Trevenen

Serbia
Dragan Milosevic
Lubica Milosevic

Slovak
Mon. John Rekem
Jana Repan

Spain
Jim Danino
Mercedes Garrido
Pili Garrido
Carmen Infante
Mercedes Lavilla
Jose Quintas
Maria Teresa Quintas
Francisco Rey
Irene Sanchez
Antonio Verdes

Sweden
Melvin Eden
Berit Eriksen
Joy Simonsen
Theodore S. Simonsen
Christina Sjöberg

Ukraine
Dr. Babick
Darcia Kopty
John Kozelko
Donna Mudlo
Cindy Pressey
Brad Richliwski
Leslie Richliwski
Bohdan Roslycky
Donald Solman
Angela Strachan

225

Index